Susan Anna Wheeler, Crosby Howard Wheeler

Grace illustrated

Or a Bouquet from our Missionary Garden

Susan Anna Wheeler, Crosby Howard Wheeler

Grace illustrated
Or a Bouquet from our Missionary Garden

ISBN/EAN: 9783337081300

Printed in Europe, USA, Canada, Australia, Japan

Cover: Foto ©ninafisch / pixelio.de

More available books at **www.hansebooks.com**

GRACE ILLUSTRATED;

OR,

A BOUQUET FROM OUR MISSIONARY GARDEN.

BY

MR. AND MRS. C. H. WHEELER,

MISSIONARIES IN HARPOOT,
EASTERN TURKEY.

"I am come into my garden, my sister, my spouse: I have gathered my myrrh with my spice."

BOSTON:
CONGREGATIONAL PUBLISHING SOCIETY,
BEACON STREET.

COPYRIGHT.
CONGREGATIONAL PUBLISHING SOCIETY.
1876.

BOSTON:
STEREOTYPED BY C. J. PETERS AND SON,
73 FEDERAL STREET.

Franklin Press: Rand, Avery, & Co., Boston.

CONTENTS.

		PAGE.
I.	A WORD WITH THE READER.	5
II.	BLIND JOHN CONCORDANCE	11
III.	BLIND DONABED	58
IV.	THE VICTORIOUS BAKER	64
V.	CRITICISM DISARMED	72
VI.	LITTLE GREGORY	77
VII.	SEED BY THE WAYSIDE	89
VIII.	DEACON HAGOP	99
IX.	THE BROKEN VOW	123
X.	ONE OF GOD'S "HIDDEN ONES"	127
XI.	THE LITTLE HUMPBACK	132
XII.	KOORDISH AMY	148
XIII.	A PILLAR REMOVED	166
XIV.	DEACON AVEDIS	173
XV.	DER KEVORK	179
XVI.	"THE LORD'S BEDROS"	190

CONTENTS.

		PAGE
XVII.	"THIEF MAGHAK".	202
XVIII.	DIVERSE GIFTS	206
XIX.	GRACE ABOUNDING	215
XX.	PATIENT SARKIS	224
XXI.	THE DESPAIRING SILVERSMITH	234
XXII.	THE KOORDISH MISSIONARY	240
XXIII.	THE LITTLE SYRIAN MAID	247
XXIV.	MISS M. E. WARFIELD	255
XXV.	THE MAN WHO MUST PREACH	262
XXVI.	OLD SARAH	268
XXVII.	BÉGO THE WIFE OF DONO	274
XXVIII.	THE AGED AUCTIONEER	282
XXIX.	PILGRIM ANNA	304

GRACE ILLUSTRATED;

or,

A BOUQUET FROM OUR MISSIONARY GARDEN.

———◆———

I.

A WORD WITH THE READER.

SINCE the enjoyment of a book by both writer and reader depends much upon their mutual good understanding, and as the aim of this little volume is liable to be misunderstood, before going out to gather our missionary nosegay, let us have a plain, frank chat about it.

Methinks I hear you asking, "Are not you the same pastor whom we saw, some twenty years ago, selecting a library for his sabbath school, and casting out from the hundred volumes before him more than a score of "Memoirs" as not worth the labor of examination? And didn't this same little wife of yours approve the deed? And do you two now put your heads and pens together to impose upon the long-suffering public a score or more of memoirs in a single volume!"

Yes, we are the same couple, and, strange as it may appear, we're of the same opinion still; and that is one reason why, fearing that our little book may fare like poor Tray at the hands of other selectors of sabbath-school libraries, we propose to protect it from unsafe company by a different name; and rightfully, for we shall aim to make it a different thing.

The purpose of these life and death sketches is not at all to immortalize certain surprisingly good little saints, or large ones, such as we used to read about in our childhood, and despairingly wish that we too might have been born such angels. For, to tell the truth, though the gospel has in some cases had wonderful power in subduing stubborn hearts here, and though Jesus has put his hands upon the heads, and by his grace touched the hearts, of some little ones, yet we have still to wait for the first saint, large or small in all our mission-field, who could equal the sample in most of those old-style memoirs. It is a gratifying though surprising fact, that, in more modern days, professedly fictitious religious writers have, while printing fiction on the titlepage, so far removed it from their delineations of the Christian life, as to give us a juster portrait of the actually existing Christian militant than had his preceding biographers. Biographical angel wings take time to grow now, and are not made to order.

We may as well confess to some perplexing questionings in fixing upon a name for our humble messenger. Nothing high-sounding or pretentious will do, of course: so we search on the common level. "Call it 'Living Stones,'" says one. But we do not feel at all in an architectural frame of mind. "'First-Fruits,' then, or 'Sheaves,'" adds a second; to which we reply, "'Handfuls' shall be the name, if any thing in that line; for the sheaves are yet to come." — "But 'Bouquet' is tame and commonplace."—"Yes, and truthful and comprehensive too; for, while it hints just the thing we wish to do, it suggests, also, the way of doing it.' We don't propose to talk of *missionary policy*, which some may think was done too exclusively in a preceding volume, nor of the missionary work in any form as seen from its human side, nor even to speak of results as such, however heart-cheering this employment might be, but only to take a quiet stroll with you, if you will, in the garden of the Lord, plucking, meanwhile, here and there a flower, a bud, a twig, a leaf, a blade of grass, as pleasant mementoes of our visit. Wearied and harassed by the toils and anxieties of even the joyous missionary work, it will be well for *us* thus to turn aside and rest a while, and not unpleasant for you to join in contemplating these more spiritual manifestations, which, though but incidental to the one great result of missions, are more potent than mere material effects to cheer and sustain the followers of Christ in the hard work of evangelism which they have to do. As our bouquet is to consist of natural flowers, not artificial, or, in other words, as the aim of these sketches is to give the reader a view of their subjects just as we have seen or are seeing them, we shall try to make the portraits true to life, even when disclosing blemishes we would gladly conceal. We shall thus gain a juster conception of the character of the missionary work, and be able more intelligently and heartily to glorify the grace that is carrying it on, when reminded that our bouquet was gathered not from the primitive paradise, but from one as yet but partially regained and restored.

II.

BLIND JOHN CONCORDANCE.

IN the spring of 1864, when our theological seminary was four years old, and the female seminary two, two equivocal candidates knocked at their doors, — a blind man and his wife from the village of Mashkir, on the Euphrates, some thirty-five miles northwest from Harpoot. The man, Hohannes ("John") by name, had in early life, like thousands in this land, lost his eyes by smallpox, and then paid, if possible, a heavier penalty for loss of sight and beauty by wedding such a wife as he could get.

The unfortunate blind man — or "Enlightened one," as the poetic sympathy of the Orient names him — who has not wealth or high reputation, must accept a wife who is at the same discount as himself, either by loss of both eyes, or of one eye plus partial want of beauty and brains, or, finally, one who has two eyes, but very little or none of the last two accomplishments. Unfortunately, Hohannes, or his friends for him, had only supplied his most sorely felt deficiency, by taking a wife with eyes only; and the result was, that the female-seminary candidate said by her first look, "To be sure, I can't learn even my *a, b, c's;* but then I can attract the attention of all by my Esquimau style of beauty." Trial had proved her truthful; and so she could not be admitted.

And what should we say to the other candidate? "Paradise Lost" and the "Iliad" witness, indeed, that pre-eminent ability may exist behind sightless eyeballs; while Milton, Socrates, and, for aught we know, old Homer too, combine to bid us beware of rejecting, without further examination, a literary aspirant because of conjugal infelicities. But, then, they do not encourage us to hope that blind men tied to uncongenial wives will be hopeful theological students. Yet Hohannes was admitted to examination, and, like Pope's traditional toad, turned out to have, beneath his far from handsome exterior, a very "precious jewel" in both head and heart. While his wonderful acquaintance with the Bible had won for him in his native village the surname of Hamapapar ("Concordance"), subsequent events showed him to be possessed of an innate power of using his acquired gift, which, in spite of all his disabilities, made him surely the most gainful candidate to the cause who ever spent two years in Harpoot Seminary, or perhaps any other, even if it does not justify "The New

York Independent" in saying, that "perhaps no man of the age has done a more important work than blind Hohannes."

Surely, at least, that brother missionary stands rebuked, who, alluding to our receiving him to the theological, and "Kohar" to the female seminary, taunted us with "receiving the lame, the halt, and the blind to our schools, because," as he said, "they are cheaper;" which reason is so far from being true, that blind students cost us more than others; and this one, at least, was worth many times what it cost to train him, and support him in the work. He left the seminary in October, 1865, and died in March, 1869; yet in that brief time he made for himself a name both in this and other lands, which will not soon die. But we have promised to be strictly truthful in painting our characters, and may as well confess here, that, stored as head and heart were with the word of truth which sanctifies the soul, he was yet apparently a good way from attaining complete sanctification. His wife complained that he didn't love her as well as he should, and died — was it from a broken heart? — not long after he entered the seminary. We are quite sure, however, that if the philosophic theory were true, which subjects the affections to the will, the poor man would have been less faulty here. But he was by no means the exemplary student we wished to see him, since he expected, and rather demanded, as a condition of obedience to the few necessary rules of the seminary, that we should imitate his habit in dealing with those whom he sought to win to the truth, and "satisfy his *conscience*" by giving chapter and verse to justify each requirement. I have sometimes imagined that there is something in the loss of the eyes which makes one unreasonably exacting. Perhaps he was thinking of the scriptural declaration in regard to bestowing more abundant honor on those members which lack, and so felt that he had a biblical claim to be petted.

He, at least, put in his claim as a blind man to be excused from compliance even with such rules as he could find no chapter and verse to invalidate. Annoyed by the fumes of new, and the stench of old tobacco-smoke elsewhere, we resolved to enjoy exemption from it on the theological premises; but "of course the rule didn't apply to a man without eyes." This notion, that no rules applied to him, was indulged to such an extent as to lead, at length, to a crisis, and a somewhat ludicrous exorcism of the troublesome spirit.

Near by the door of the theological seminary was that of the female-seminary harem, over which all Oriental customs and prejudices, as well as our own promise to parents to leave to *them* their daughters' matrimonial arrangements, compelled us to write, " Taboo to lovers and love-letters." Hohannes' inability to love satisfactorily her who had died did not prevent him from being insnared by the sweet tones of the assistant teacher, into whose hands, by lying in wait at the forbidden door, he one day succeeded in slipping, not the usual romantic nonsense, but a plain, outspoken epistle on the business in hand; and, having done this, he waited somewhat impatiently for the expected reply, little suspecting that she, as in duty bound, had handed the letter unread to her superiors. So when, a few days later, the students were sent forth, two and two, for a brief vacation preaching-tour, and Hohannes' name was not read with the rest, to his prompt inquiry, " And where shall I go ? " came the reply, " You, brother, can stay here, and attend to your matrimonial affairs."

The Harpoot parsonage was then in building, and a man needed to sift dirt for mortar: so when Hohannes added, "But how shall I earn my bread?" we replied, "If you feel penitent enough over that love-letter, we suggest that you do it by sitting in dust and ashes, and using that sieve." He did it; but the joke leaked out, and from that day to this there have been no more liers-in-wait at the tabooed door.

During his "short course" of two years, Hohannes made more than average progress in his studies, which were, exegesis of Scripture, theology, and preaching, and graduated with his class in 1865. He had meanwhile manifested much shrewdness and enthusiasm in evangelistic labor in the vicinity, frequently succeeding, partly from the fact of his blindness, but mostly from his natural sagacity, in gaining access to Armenian churches. He was specially skillful in silencing opponents, chiefly by a ready and dexterous use of Scripture, but often by an adroit turning of his antagonist's weapons against himself. A single incident will illustrate this latter trait. The priest of a certain village frequently visited by the students had a trick of asking them whether they had studied a certain branch of knowledge, of which he was, doubtless, even more ignorant than most of them, and then, on their confessing that they had not, turning to the people, who knew not even the name of the wonderful study, with the triumphant inquiry whether a man so ignorant as that was fit to preach the gospel. When several unfortunate theologues had in this way been worsted, Hohannes started for the place, declaring that he would silence the wily priest. So, having committed to memory a long list of authors who have treated on the old man's favorite study, he replied to the usual question by glibly rattling off those authors' names, and inquiring to which of them he referred. It was now the priest's turn to bear the laugh; and he never again dared attack a Protestant preacher.

Hohannes' blindness, of course, caused him much inconvenience in getting about, sometimes even when he had companions. Once, in a hilly region, his two fellow-travelers left him for a moment, going in different directions to decide on the correct road, and, on their return, could find no Hohannes, but at length tracked his mule down a very steep hillside, into a ravine, at the bottom of which, on one side they discovered the animal, and on the other his master. When left alone, the mule, with something of his rider's originality of purpose, decided to choose a path for himself, and, spite of all his opposition, had carried him off. Finding that the beast was taking him down such a road, and resolved not to be lost, even if the mule was, he had slipped off to wait the issue of events.

But, in spite of obstacles, his zeal and energy carried him on, resolved to accomplish feats of travel and evangelism deemed difficult even for men with eyes. Among other things, learning of the darkened condition of the Armenians in Russia, he resolved, at all risks, to visit and supply them with portions of the Scriptures. So he ordered a box made of thick boards, so hollowed out by mortising, that he might fill the cavities with very thin copies of the separate Gospels, and thus take them, undiscovered, across the border. But by our advice this plan was given up; and, shortly after graduation, he went to Shèpik, a wretched little village of some forty houses, about fifty miles north-west from Harpoot, in which was a church whose pastor's lack of energy had put to sleep that small part of the people who adhered to him, and so deprived himself of all support.

When he appealed to the Evangelical Union for aid, they advised him to leave for a time, and go to a hostile village and get roused up, and invite Hohannes to come and wake up his people. He went; and, when the people met him with lamentations over poor crops and poverty, he bade them begin their lamentations at another place, and remove the cause by repaying God that of which they had robbed him. Then taking for his text, "Bring ye all the tithes into the storehouse," &c. (Mal. iii. 10), he enforced the duty of paying into the Lord's treasury one-tenth of all their earnings.

His sermon we reserve to be reported as subsequently preached in the Harpoot pulpit; but its immediate fruit in Shèpik was remarkable.[1] The pastor was called back to find a different church from the one he left. Would that as great a change might have been wrought in his good but sluggish nature! But Hohannes' work went on. The little mustard-seed, thus sowed in this insignificant village, soon became a tree of so wide-spreading branches, that multitudes of churches and communities in this and other lands rested under the shade, and partook of the fruit of it. In the hard struggle to lead the people out of the Egyptian bondage of dependence on foreign aid, and introduce self-support, and consequent independence, among the churches, we missionaries had apparently reached a Red Sea, through which God only could open a way to go forward; and by the hand of this humble man he did it, and we were soon

[1] Those wishing to do so can find the particulars in chap. x. of "Ten Years on the Euphrates."

singing songs of deliverance on the other side of the flood. We have not, indeed, yet crossed the Jordan, and begin to fear that our sins may deprive some of us of the privilege of leading the people into the goodly land by completing in our field the work to be done here by the American churches. This is not the place to go into particulars of results of the tithing movement, the good fruits of which are increasing with the advance of time. While no attempt is made to constrain persons, church-members or others, to pay tithes, yet the feeling is becoming more and more widespread, that while the giving of this exact proportion of income is not divinely fixed as an invariable rule for all, and while each person may decide for himself to what special department of Christian expenditure he will appropriate his tithes, yet the system offers the simplest and most practicable method of providing for evangelistic expense, and is at the same time most beneficial spiritually to the contributor. Though the sermon of Hohannes, as reported by Miss West for "The Missionary Herald," of October, 1868, has been scattered by tens of thousands of copies over England and America, it may profitably find a place here. We give, of course, only a brief abstract. Blind men don't write their sermons, nor even preach from notes. Miss West says, " I wish you could have seen for yourself how interested the people were in the discourse. The blindness of the preacher added to the interest. Saying, 'We will *read*' such a 'chapter' or 'hymn,' he would repeat the same, word for word. When he called upon the people to read, it was for their sake rather than his own; and, when the reader had reached just the point he desired, he never failed to say, 'Stop,' that he might take it up just there.

"He began by repeating that striking passage, 'Will a man rob God? Yet ye have robbed me. But ye say, Wherein have we robbed thee? In tithes and offerings,' &c. (Mal. iii. 8–10.) He then, in few words, told us that he proposed to show from the word of God that giving a tenth to the Lord was a primitive institution, attended with great benefits and blessings to the givers, and perpetuated and enforced under the *new dispensation* no less than the old. 'Open your Bibles,' said he, 'at the fourteenth chapter of Genesis, and let some one read the eighteenth and twentieth verses.' Bibles were instantly opened all over the house, and the passage read in clear tones by one of the congregation. 'Abraham gave tithes to Melchizedek,' said the preacher, 'more than four hundred years before the giving of the law to Moses,—Abraham, "the father of the faithful," whose children the Jews glory in being,—Abraham, whom even Moslems honor, and call "the blessed." Now turn to the twenty-eighth chapter, and read the twentieth, twenty-first and twenty-second verses.' Jacob's vow was read, concluding with the words, 'And of all that thou shalt give me, I will surely give the tenth unto thee.' He then rapidly drew the contrast between Jacob's *going* to Padan-aram,—alone, and in utter destitution,—and the *return*, with his flocks and herds, and camels, menservants and maid-servants; for, in spite of Laban's covetousness, the man had increased greatly. 'And now,' he said, 'open at the twenty-seventh of Leviticus, and read the thirtieth verse. "And all the *tithe* of the land *is the Lord's*,"' repeated the preacher. 'Nine-tenths for yourselves; but one-tenth "is holy unto the Lord." Open at Numbers eighteenth, and read the twentieth, twenty-first, twenty-sixth, twenty-eighth and twenty-ninth verses.' This was done; and then Hohannes briefly commented on each verse. He said the Levites, who ministered in the house of the Lord, were to have no part or inheritance in the *land;* for the *tithes* of the people were to be their inheritance; and of these tithes *they* were to offer a *tenth* to the Lord, ' even of all the *best* thereof.' 'Read Deut. xiv. 22, and xxvi. 12. See the abundant provision made, not only for the Levites, but also for the " stranger, the fatherless, and the widow." Read, also, 2 Chron. xxxi. 4–10, where the people are described as obeying the command of God, and bringing in " abundantly " of the " increase of the land." And the chief priest answered King Hezekiah, when he questioned him concerning the " *heaps:*" " Since the people began to bring the offerings into the house of the Lord, we have had enough to eat, and have left plenty; *for the Lord hath blessed his people;* and that which is left is this great store." Now read Neh. xiii. 10, 13, and 14. Mark the contrast! The people no longer gave tithes: the house of the Lord was desecrated; and the Levites had forsaken their sacred office, and "*fled*, every one to *his own* FIELD."

"'And now,' continued the preacher, 'we will turn to the new dispensation. Open at the twenty-third of Matthew, and read the twenty-third verse: "These *ought* ye to have done, and *not* to leave the other undone," are our blessed Saviour's words to the scribes and Pharisees. Ye do well to pay *tithes:* it is your duty. But ye ought also to do judgment, mercy and faith. Now turn to Luke xi. 42: "Woe unto you Pharisees! for ye tithe . . . all manner of herbs, and pass over judgment and the love of God: *these ought* ye to *have done*, and not to leave the other undone." Read Luke iii. 7–12: "Bring forth fruits *worthy* of *repentance*,"' repeated the preacher. 'John the Baptist was a connecting link between the Jewish and the gospel dispensations; and he spake as he was moved by the Spirit of God. "Now, also, the ax is laid at the *root* of the tree." What tree? It was nothing less than the tree — the root — of self and selfishness.

"'What this good fruit is he tells us in the eleventh verse: "He that hath two coats, let him impart to him that hath none; and he that hath meat [food], let him do likewise." Where, now, remains the tenth?' he exclaimed. 'Under the new dispensation, not one-*tenth* merely, but one-HALF, is required.' (At this announcement, there was an evident sensation in the audience, many a face lighting up with a smile, as the electric current shot through the assembly.)

"The preacher continued, 'Read now the sixth of Luke, thirty-eighth verse: "Give, and it shall be given unto you." *Give* and you *shall have wherewith* to *give.* Shut your hand and your heart, and you shut the windows of heaven; you keep back the blessing of God. See what Christ says in Luke xii. 33: " Sell that ye have, and give alms," &c., which means, consider yourselves as *stewards* of God's grace on the earth, seeking your inheritance in the world to come. You are to set light store by your earthly possessions, and lay up treasure in heaven. Now read Luke xiv. 33.' Slowly and solemnly the preacher repeated the words of the Master: '" So, likewise, who soever he be of you that *forsaketh not* ALL that he hath, he CAN NOT be my disciple.' Ah, my brethren,' said he, ' it is not merely a *tenth,* or even a *half,* of our worldly possessions, that Christ claims: *it is our* ALL ! Think upon the meaning of those words. It is thus he speaks to you: If you wish to be my disciple, you must *count the cost.* You can not serve two masters. You must give up every thing that the children of this world seek after. You must hold yourselves *aloof* from your earthly possessions' [such is the Armenian version of Luke xiv. 33], 'holding to them *loosely,* setting your affections on things above. Your comfort, pleasure, honor, ease, yea, your *very life,* you must esteem as nothing in comparison with my service. And in thus losing *all,* you will find all, and that for ever.

"'Open your Bibles at Matt. xix. 29, and Mark x. 29, and read the glorious promise to those who truly "*forsake all*" for Christ and his cause. See!' exclaimed Hohannes, after solemnly repeating the passage,—'see how rich the reward! a hundred-fold in this life, and *life everlasting* beside! Now open at Luke nineteenth, and read from the second to the tenth verse. Note the words of Zaccheus,

"The half of my goods I give to the poor," and mark the answer of our Saviour. But what say you? Is salvation to be *bought with money?* We all know that it is " without money, without price." Why, then, this blessing upon Zaccheus?'—' Because,' answered one of the congregation, ' the *giving* was the fruit of his *faith*.' —' Yes,' rejoined the preacher, ' Zaccheus brought forth fruit worthy of true repentance, and immediately received the promised blessing.

"'Now let me tell you a story. When I was in the class in sermonizing, in the seminary, our teacher was very anxious that we who were soon to go forth as preachers, and perhaps become pastors, should work upon right principles; and he often talked to us of our duty as leaders to teach the people to do for themselves. He sometimes told us of places where much money (of the Board) had been expended by missionaries, and but little real good accomplished, because the people had not been taught to give for Christ's cause. "In one little village," he said, "forty thousand piasters" [sixteen hundred dollars] "of the Board's money was spent; the people only giving fifty piasters during thirteen years. And the work in that place amounts to nothing to-day, because of this unwise course." It so happened, that, when my course of study was finished, I was appointed to that village. It was the last place I should have chosen. I had no desire to go to that field; but God had so ordered, and I went. The missionaries told me that my wages would be fifteen hundred piasters per year, of which the people were to pay six hundred; and, before I left, one of them took me aside, and counseled me to make it as easy for the people as possible, by eating at their houses, &c., because it would come hard to them at *first* to do so much.

"'Soon after I went there, a neighboring pastor came over to the village, and we held a meeting with the brethren. We talked about my support; and it seemed that they had, with much difficulty, subscribed five hundred piasters per year. I told them the missionaries had said they would pay six hundred. "*Never!*" they exclaimed. "We cannot raise another *para*" [one-fortieth of a piaster]. And pastor M—— said it was impossible; they were too poor. "Where, then, shall I get my other hundred?" I asked. "We will help you from our place," he replied.

"'But my mind was not at rest. That night I thought much on the subject. I said to myself, "Suppose the American Board should one day withdraw its support from this and other feeble churches, what will become of them?" And I prayed, "O thou who knowest all things, and with whom are all plans, show thy ignorant servant how thy kingdom can best be established in this land." And it seemed to me that a voice said in my soul, "It can be done by *giving one in every ten.*" When I thought it over, it occurred to me to test it first in my own case. One-tenth of my fifteen hundred per year would be one hundred and fifty piasters. "No," I said, "I can't give so much as that: I should suffer for it." But, when I took it out of every month's salary, it did not seem so much. "One-tenth of my one hundred twenty five will be twelve piasters and a half. *I can do it,*" I said, "and I *will,* even if I do have to pinch a little." It happened that pastor —— visited us about that time, and I laid the subject before him. "It can be done," he said; "and it must be. I will give a tenth of my salary." And so said preacher ——, who also came over. "Well, then,"

I said, "do you think it will do for me to lay it before the brethren?"—"Yes," they replied: "it is the best thing you can do."

"'So I prepared myself, and preached to the people on the next sabbath. The Lord blessed his own word. They accepted it, and came together to be "written" for their tithes. When we made a rough estimate, it appeared that their *tenths* would exceed my entire salary. "Why, how is this?" they all said. "It was so hard before! but now it comes very easy, and it is truly pleasant."

"'Now, to show you how God blessed that little flock, I will mention one case. One brother had a vegetable-garden, which the Turkish official, in assessing the tax, had estimated at nine hundred piasters for that year's produce, taxing him ninety piasters. Others said it was too much: it would not produce that amount. But mark the fulfillment of the promise in Mal. iii. 10. That brother sold three thousand piasters' worth of vegetables from that garden, besides what was eaten by a household of thirty-two persons, and given away; amounting to full three thousand more. Others were also blessed; and all acknowledged that they had never known a year of such prosperity. The people not only supported their preacher and school-teacher, but also paid over two thousand piasters for other purposes.

"The preacher was about to close his discourse, when a member of the congregation arose, and asked permission to say a few words. 'I have learned,' he said, 'from one of the missionaries another truth, which has great weight in this giving of one-tenth of our income to the Lord. Under the old dispensation, the Jews were only required to care for their own nation; but, under the new dispensation, the command is, "Go ye into all the world, and preach the gospel to every creature." Therefore a *tenth* is not enough for Christians to give.

"To this, the teacher responded, 'A *tenth* is the very *least* that a disciple of Christ can give. Over and above that, he should give as God prospers him. And now,' he added, 'let us seek the aid of the Holy Spirit, that we, and all our offerings, may find acceptance before God.'"

To this report, Miss West adds, "It is difficult to do justice to a scene and a sermon so unique. When that sightless man was led up into the pulpit, his appearance was any thing but attractive. He looked rough, and uncared-for, quite inferior in person. But he had a message from the Lord of hosts; and well did he deliver it, reminding one of the words, 'God hath chosen the weak things of the world to confound the things which are mighty; and base things of the world, and things which are despised, hath God chosen,' &c. It was worth much to see and hear one who had been so evidently taught of the Spirit, and made the honored instrument of laying a new foundation-stone for the building of Christ's church throughout the world. For the new ray of light that dawned in that obscure village of Armenia two years since has begun to radiate from many distant points; and we believe that it will solve the problem of the support of Christian institutions in all lands, and hasten the day when the earth shall be filled with the glory of God. Well may every worker in foreign lands say with Jesus, 'I thank thee, O Father, Lord of heaven and earth, because thou hast hid these things from the wise and prudent, and revealed them unto babes. Even so, Father, for so it seemed good in thy sight.'"

With his restless longing to preach the gospel in regions beyond, Hohannes had resolved to go to Moosh Plain, a week's journey east of Harpoot, of the ignorant and wretched condition of the Armenian inhabitants of which he had heard from missionaries and native pastors who had visited it the year before; and, at the date of preaching this sermon (May 3, 1868), he, with another missionary volunteer like himself, was on his way thither.

Reaching the place, his companion, now Pastor Garabed of Haboosie, was located in the city of Moosh; but Hohannes went to what we may hope was the most wretched spot of that pre-eminently wretched district, the village of Havadoric. Mr. Cole of Erzroom, who visited the place in 1872, thus writes of it: "It is a village of some fifty houses, situated half a mile up a steep mountain-side, where it overlooks most of the great Moosh Plain. We saw tokens of abject poverty in the whole region, but in this village more than all. We visited the people at their homes; and such dingy, dirty, dark abodes for human beings, I have never seen in Turkey. In all the village were only two guest-rooms, — raised places in the corner of a stable, inclosed by a low mud-wall, to separate guests from the cattle. Others have nothing but the poorest kind of '*doon*,' a sort of sheep-pen affair, windowless, with only a hole in the top to let the smoke out. And in these hovels, such poverty! As to clothing, I should say there was nothing you could dignify by that title, — mere tattered rags hanging from shivering forms. As cold weather comes on, many of the children must stay in doors to keep from freezing. At night, when you and I lie down in our soft, warm beds, think of their lying down upon the cold, hard ground, with a few squalid rags for their bed of down."

Of the Moosh Plain itself, Mr. H. N. Barnum, who visited it in 1867, wrote, "This plain is about sixty miles long, and ten or twelve wide, and contains about seventy nominally Christian villages. More than a week were we detained; and I question whether Providence did not detain us that we might see and feel more deeply the wants of that region. It was now genuine winter weather; yet I think I never saw anywhere else, not even in the warm sunshine of Egypt, so much nakedness, total or partial. Adults, of course, had the semblance of clothing, though it was often a mass of rags and shreds sewed or tied together. But the poor children! It makes my heart ache to think of them. Some had a tolerably whole shirt and drawers; and some had no drawers, and what was once a shirt was now a few shreds hanging from the shoulders. Many had only a rag on the shoulders, as a sort of jacket, with holes to put the arms through; and others had not a thread upon their bodies. The people seem to be almost wholly destitute of beds. Wherever we went, we found that the beds were a piece of carpet, or felt, or coarse straw-matting, or a little straw, with a piece of carpet as a covering. In six or seven villages which we visited, we did not notice a woman or a child who had either stockings or shoes for the feet. They walked about in the snow and mud, and over the frozen ground, with bare feet. Our pastors had never seen destitution like this, and it made a deep impression upon them. And the spiritual condition of the people is as bad as the physical. In the three or four monasteries surrounding the plain, there are said to be fifty *vartabeds*, men of more or less education. What a work they might do in these seventy villages, in improving the condition of the people, if they only had the heart for it! But they are in a great measure responsible for this state of things. They come down periodically from their haunts of dissipation, and gather up and carry off whatever the people can spare; and this has helped to discourage the people, and repress enterprise. *The great want now is the pure gospel.* This will not only save their souls, it will give them true civilization and refinement. To us the people seemed ripe for the reception of the truth. They are growing tired of the yoke, and are beginning to murmur against it. The pastors turned away from Moosh Plain with the determination to induce the Harpoot Evangelical Union, if consistent with the work undertaken in Koordistan, to do something for the Moosh district. May the Lord strengthen them for it!" If Mr. Barnum's pen, by a more vivid picturing of the poverty and degradation of the inhabitants of the plain below, seems to dispute the pre-eminence in wretchedness of Havadoric, we must remember that Mr. Barnum spent a cheerless, stormy winter's week on the Plain, while Mr. Cole saw the mountaineers only in their summer Sunday's best. Mr. Knapp gives an inlook upon an additional element of Havadoric degradation. "As I sat talking with the villagers about the necessity of educating their sons and *daughters*, I noticed a couple of the latter coming tugging up the exceedingly steep mountain, each with a ponderous load of brushwood and roots on her back, which had been gathered on the adjoining hills. As they came up, and threw their loads down near my feet, an old man turned round, and pointing to them, — down whose faces the perspiration flowed, while they were panting for breath,— exclaimed, 'Educate our *daughters!* Why, if we should do that, *who would bring our wood?*'"

To the work, then, in this metropolis of Turkey darkness and degradation, our missionary devoted himself. But hardly had he reached his field when he gained his most coveted prize — was he in error who said missionaries always fare so? — by getting a first-rate wife. Visiting the city of Bitlis, he met a pupil of the female seminary, who had rejected desirable offers of marriage, but, in spite of the opposition of friends, at once accepted Mr. Concordance, saying, "No matter if he is homely and blind, he's a Christian; and I'll marry him."

And thus, apparently, had Providence not only provided him with eyes, but the ignorant *daughters* of the village with an educator.

The story of their labors must, of course, be very brief; for Hohannes reached his field late in 1868, and died March 31, 1869. Mr. Knapp says of them, "They were doing a great work there." Sure we may be, that such a man, united to such a woman, could do nothing less than a *great* work, even when shut up in so *small* a field of action. Just how much of the striking spiritual work in that village was due to their labors, and how much to those of another "devotedly Christian helper," Arakial — Apostle — by name, who had made his grave in that stricken village, we can not say. But the impress of one or both is indelibly stamped upon the people. A colporter who visited the place but a few days before the death of Hohannes, and while he was, with his characteristic earnestness, laboring to rouse and enlighten the people, reported the village as "a heaven on earth." Wrote Mr.

ARMENIAN PRIEST

Knapp, in the same letter whose postscript told of the death of Ilohannes, "In that village of forty houses, where a few years since the people were notorious for being robbers and murderers, like their Koordish neighbors, (how changed now!) there are sixty just learning to read, some of whom are upwards of *eighty* years of age." And while doing his utmost for his little flock, among whom his influence almost obliterated the distinction between Armenian and Protestant, he forgot not to labor for the spread of the tithing principle. Writes Mr. Knapp, " He earnestly besought us to throw our influence in favor of the tithing system. And he *practiced* what he preached. His salary was only eight dollars a month; and, although he had a wife and a lad to support from this, he gave without fail one-tenth into the 'storehouse,' thus leaving seven dollars and twenty cents for the monthly support of himself and family." When seized with the fatal illness, which lasted but three or four days, he at once expressed the opinion that he should die, and made such arrangements as he could for the future comfort of his wife. Much of the time on his death-bed was spent in giving counsel to his little flock. So calm was he, and so confident of his approaching end, that he gave special directions for his burial, and had himself clothed with the apparel in which he wished to be interred!

When his fellow-missionary went from Moosh for the burial-services, he expected, that, as uniformly happens in similar cases elsewhere, the Armenians would manifest hostility. But, instead of doing so, they vied with the Protestants in carrying out to the letter Hohannes' particular requests in regard to his burial; carrying him to *their own cemetery*, and seeming to be as genuine mourners as his own people.

Such love had but four months of actual labor among them inspired among this simple-hearted people! A few months later a little company, accompanied by Mr. Knapp, gathered for the formation of a church among them. Mr. Knapp shall tell his own story of the scene. "The greatest feast of good things we enjoyed in Havadoric. Our own people" [of Bitlis] "had observed a day of fasting and prayer for the village, the villagers also observing the same day; and the presence of the Holy Spirit was manifest. The worshiping congregation was in tears before God, and a number were converted. On the night of our arrival, we called together eighteen of the most prominent men; and each one, in reply to the question whether he desired a church to be formed, replied, 'Badvelly, I believe there ought to be a church; but *I* am not worthy to be admitted to it.'

"On a following day we spent ten hours in examining twenty-two persons. Their history and religious experience were exceedingly interesting, and most stimulating to one's piety. Their piety is characterized by *simplicity*.

"One, when brought under conviction, was in great distress in view of his past life. A notorious thief and robber, he with others had stolen from the flocks in many villages, often appropriating to himself but a small portion of the slaughtered prey, leaving the rest to be devoured by wild beasts. In one of the prayer-meetings he stated this fact, saying it would take half the village was worth to replace what he had stolen, and with tearful entreaty seeking forgiveness. They promptly replied, 'Brother, we most cheerfully forgive you. Go to the other villages, and confess your thefts and seek forgiveness; and if they demand restitution, as you are poor, we will help you pay the debt.' Another said he had defrauded government of taxes to the amount of five piasters (twenty cents), and he did not find forgiveness from God until he resolved to refund the amount.

"One of two brothers, partners in business, had stolen a sheep from a Turk fifteen years ago. When brought under conviction, he went and confessed the theft; but the haughty Turk would not forgive him on his restoring the sheep, but demanded what would have accrued as the product of that sheep during the fifteen years. In great distress, he went and confessed all to his brother also, and asked what he should do. The brother replied, 'Let us pray over it; and, if the Turk adhere to his demand, we must refund the whole as he requires.'

"They prayed, after which the man again sought forgiveness; and, to his happy surprise, the Turk released him on his paying the sheep."

Suffice it to say that a church of nine male and two female members was formed, the "delegates" from abroad being "surprised at the simplicity of faith and strength of Christian character of the two latter." "And now" — April, 1870 — "seventeen houses, or one hundred and fifty souls, in the village, are Protestant; and the whole village, five persons excepted, are persuaded of the truth. Of the Protestants, sixteen promise tithes to the Lord. All the male members of the church but one give tithes."

Well might Mr. Knapp add, "What a change has come over this village of Havadoric!" and "the 28th" of April, 1870, "was, I think, the happiest day of my life."

In the autumn of 1871 Mr. Cole of Erzroom visited the place with Mr. Knapp, when a simple epitaph was engraved to his memory upon the flat stone that marks the grave of Hohannes, of whom he remarks, "The noble man seems to have left his imprint on the village." "Those," says he, "were happy days that we spent among that poverty-stricken people. We found them so earnest, so rich in faith, many of them, that we thought little of the surroundings. The sabbath, what a precious day it was to us all! A full house of such eager, earnest listeners — who could help preaching the gospel to them! Their very presence seemed to be mouth, tongue, utterance, to the speaker.

"Of the three exercises of the day, one most of all touched my heart, and that because of a single incident, which, perhaps better than any thing else, illustrates the utter poverty of the people. One of the eighteen members of the church presented his young babe for the seal of the covenant. It was too much. The tears went coursing down my cheeks in spite of me. I thought of the English consul's little boy, whom we had recently baptized in Erzroom, of the elegant baptismal robe that had come all the way from England to grace the occasion.

"But here was a son of the faith, whose sole costume would hardly be considered a fit contribution to the *kitchen mop* in the Western world,— a mere bundle of old tattered rags! Thank God, I said, their robes will be all one 'up there.'"

True, brother, and yet not true. We query whether, "up there," some of these humble ones, with the poor blind man who "pointed the way" thither, will not wear richer robes and brighter crowns than many of the great ones of the earth.

God does not set his jewels here.
Earth's shining ore, treasure of worldly great,
Wherewith bedecked they walk in pride abroad,
Will be but pavement for the gorgeous courts,
Where, freed from all which weights and clogs them here,

Clothed in the forms of heaven's own lustrous life,
Endowed with affluence all unknown on earth,
And robed in raiment brighter than the light,
His chosen ones shall walk erect with him,
The difference all " discerned "
' Twixt those who serve him, those who serve him
    not.
When earth, with all its pomp and power and pride,
Shall fade and sink in the great final fire,
His own, his jewels, spared from every harm,
Who, scorned of men, oft to each other spake,
Who prayed and toiled in pain and weakness here,
Winning the wandering to the way of life,
Shall shine as stars for ever and for ever.
Their glorious setting then shall be
The glittering crown upon the head of Him
Who bought them with his blood.

III.

BLIND DONABED.

SOME eight years since, a poor blind beggar in Hoghi — there are multitudes of such in this land — was induced to attend a Bible-class opened by the Protestant pastor, and to commit to memory some verses of Scripture. Not long after, he obtained a copy of a primer for the blind, which he soon mastered; and purchased all the books which were to be found in Armenian in that character, — the thirty-fourth and eighty-sixth Psalms, and the third chapter of John.

It was soon proved by practical illustration, that "the entrance of thy words giveth light: it giveth understanding unto the simple." Though now the poor blind man has Matthew entire to read, and has good ear acquaintance with many parts of the Bible, it is deeply interesting to hear him give enthusiastic expression to his love for those "two psalms," which his fingers first read. "More to be desired are they than gold, yea, than much fine gold, sweeter also than honey and the honeycomb," seems to him almost too tame to tell the preciousness of those two chapters. He soon "tasted, and saw that the Lord is good, and blessed is the man that trusteth in him."

Our first acquaintance with him was at a visit to Hoghi, some four years since, when, in a prayer-meeting, our attention was attracted to his earnest and really eloquent prayer, in which he was specially drawn out for the missionaries, that God by his Spirit would "sustain, comfort, and cheer those who, for his sake, have left home, country, and friends, and in their loneliness need so much that comfort which comes from on high."

We began to query whether here might not be a successor to "Blind John Concordance."

Having, by inquiry, satisfied ourselves of the integrity of his Christian character, we, a year afterwards, admitted him to the normal school. At the door of the school a difficulty arose. With a face full of sorrow, he informed us that he was thirty piasters ($1.25) in debt. His begging income, less the tithes paid into the Lord's treasury, had been less by this amount than his expenses for the year past.

A "farewell begging-tour" of ten minutes, taken by our leave among ourselves, settled that matter; and he entered the school free from debt, receiving for his support four cents a day from the missionary treasury. Let no one exclaim against the meanness of this sum, till informed, that having lived upon it for six months, and spent the succeeding winter vacation in labor on a salary of two dollars per month, he, the following year, gave up in despair, and went back to self-support at his old trade, when told, that, fearing students lived too poorly on their allowance, we had decided to feed them at a table of our own providing. "During the past year his four cents a day had sufficed for food and shoes; and what should he do now for shoes?"

Let no one here propose to condemn him for going back again to begging, which is in this land a usual and honorable profession for "enlightened men."

But our candidate is back again, having meantime fared better than did poor John Concordance, by getting a wife with a fair amount of brains plus one eye, and who has been received to the female seminary. Protestant Christian blind men have a prospect of faring better matrimonially than have their predecessors. Whether this one will prove to be a worthy successor of him of Mashkir, we know not. Sure we are, that while, like him, he will, by the mere fact of his loss of sight, find access to some else inaccessible, and while, by his simple, earnest piety, he will be fitted to do good, he is not, like John, a semi-son of thunder, and so can not make the stir in the world which he did.

Should he, a thing not improbable, finally prove himself unsuited for systematic evangelistic labor, and backslide into his old business, sure I am that the comparatively insignificant sum spent on his Bible training will pay as a missionary investment; for, going with open mouth as he did, from Marash on the south, to the Anti-Taurus range on the north, he can not fail to drop much precious gospel seed, some of which must fall into good ground. He now goes out, with a salary increased to five dollars, to labor for a time, perhaps permanently, in Komk, one of the wickedest towns among the many wicked ones in our mission-field.

We ask on his behalf the prayers of each Christian reader.

IV.

THE VICTORIOUS BAKER.

SOME twelve years ago, when the doctrines and demands of the newly arrived gospel were in the mouths of many who had it not, — and in this way Christ was practically preached by many who were experimentally ignorant of him, — a baker in Yegheki, Melcone by name, became roused to the question, whether it was not his duty to keep the sabbath holy, and his privilege to enjoy one day of rest in seven.

Calling upon a priest to decide the question, he was at first informed that to bake and sell bread on the sabbath is sin; and then, again, changing sides, the priest comforted him by saying, "It is lawful to do good on the sabbath day; and baking is a good and necessary work." The command, "Remember the sabbath day to keep it holy," still ringing in his ears, he called upon a second priest, who assured him that he was doing no wrong. But, as he says, the more men said, "Go on with your baking," the more it appeared to him that he must conform literally to God's command; and he decided to close his bakery on the sabbath. Feeling that in so doing he had done a good thing, he had a not unnatural feeling of satisfaction, slightly tinged with Phariseeism. In these circumstances, he one day found in a neighbor's house a primer, which, as he says, "opened of itself to the passage," which, after much effort, he spelled out, "'Be thou in the fear of the Lord all the day long.'" He had supposed his duty all done, and himself safe, in stopping bread-baking on the sabbath; but here was a new command, which at once condemned him as a sinner. Borrowing the little book, he conned it day after day in search of more light, and at length decided to go at once to the fountain head, by purchasing the Protestant Testament. This done, he tremblingly went to the neighboring town of Mezereh, and to the newly opened Protestant place of worship there.

Ere long he had courage to visit the Protestant preacher in his own town, and finally to attend a meeting there on the sabbath. Spies, whom the priests kept on the watch, at once reported the fact; and when, at evening, he appeared in church, his name was read on the list of those whom the priest cursed for adhering to the Protestants, forbidding all persons to speak to, or to have any dealings with, them.

This was just the thing needed to make him decide, once for all, to waver no longer. He at once rose and went forward, and demanded by what right these curses were heaped upon him for reading a book which differs in no respect from the Testament on the altar, except in being in the modern, spoken tongue. And, having shown that the priest had been acting contrary to the spirit of their own Scriptures, he added, "Though I was not a Protestant, I become such now. I go out of the church-doors, and write upon them that I belong here no longer." And he was as good as his word. Henceforth he adhered to the little company of despised, persecuted ones. And now began his trials in the effort to keep the sabbath. Those who would gladly have had him close his bakery on the sabbath, that their own trade might increase, resolved now to prevent it, and complained of him as a person who caused the people inconvenience by closing his bakery one day in seven.

He was summoned before the pasha, and commanded to keep his shop open on all days. He pleaded his Christian faith as a reason for declining, but was told that other Christians baked and sold bread on the sabbath, and he must do so. He was cast into prison, and retained there a day, but, remaining immovable, was finally discharged; the pasha concluding to let him have his own way. Another and another effort was made through successive pashas, with the same result, till at length, after a four-years' struggle, his enemies joined hands for a final effort, and he was summoned before the council, and bidden in the most peremptory manner to keep his bakery open permanently. His answer was prompt and decisive. Telling them that his religion forbade him to continue his usual occupation on God's day, he added, "Though all the world unite in effort to compel me to violate my conscience, and I be forced to beg my bread; though you beat me, imprison me, and even take off my head, — I shall be of the same mind. I will not profane the sabbath." — "Close your bakery then," they replied. "Give me a paper," he replied, "certifying that you compel me to do this because of my adherence to my faith, so that all persons may know the reason of my punishment, and I will do as you bid." They declining to do this, he returned to his bakery, and took his seat upon the elevated platform from which customers are supplied, ready to continue his business, but was soon followed by an officer, who bade him close his doors, and surrender the keys. "Here I sit, and shall sit till removed by force," was his reply. The officer, astonished at courage so unusual, returned for further instructions from his superiors, who said, "You need not use force." He returned, and said to Melcone, "Bake on: I am instructed to let you alone." And from that day to this his victory has been complete. Nobody now imagines that he can be compelled to bake or sell bread on the sabbath.

When the same officer was sent to command some butchers to keep open shop on the sabbath, and they began to plead conscientious scruples, he replied, "You'll not get off by that sort of easy, timid talk. If you expect to succeed, you must, like Melcone the baker, take your lives in your hands, and say, 'We will not.'" Hearing of Melcone's success, the Armenian bakers resolved to follow his example.

But the stuff reformers are made of was not in them. Summoned before the pasha, and attempting to plead conscientious scruples, they encountered only ridicule. "You talk of conscience!" exclaimed the ruler, — "you who manifest such scruples nowhere else. Melcone shows clearly by all his conduct that he has a conscience; and you, that you are only pretending to have one. Stop your foolish talk, and get you to your work; and, if I have any more trouble from you, you shall be suitably punished."

To their work they went, and gave the pasha no more trouble.

Melcone is now the chief baker in this city, and known by all as a God-fearing man.

And he is no less bold and uncompromising in practical Christian work, ready to do for Christ whatever his hand finds to do.

Would that all Christians, like him, having succeeded in getting new-comers into the house of God on the sabbath, would, like him, at the close of service, take them aside to talk and pray with them in hope of savingly impressing their minds with the truth they have heard.

With even a few such faithful, earnest workers in every church, the millennial day would not long delay its dawning.

V.

CRITICISM DISARMED.

THE man who disarmed it was one who, in all preliminary action, threatened to make himself its victim; but he is first to be introduced to the reader.

Some score of years ago, a boy in Diarbekir, Geragose by name, and called, from his father's business, Hoharrarian, (son of the) "Cook," attached himself to the gospel party. Such was his father's rage on hearing the fact, that, seizing his carving-knife, he ran to seek his son, declaring he would kill him on the spot. Fleeing to the house of the missionary, the boy lay concealed till his father's wrath had sufficiently subsided to allow him to come forth. The father died not long after; and in due time the son, grown now to manhood, and desiring to enter the ministry, appeared at the door of our Harpoot Theological Seminary, and was admitted; his wife also entering the female seminary. With a personal appearance not very prepossessing, his face quite badly pitted by small-pox, and a somewhat hesitating utterance, he excited no brilliant hopes for his future. As a scholar, he was not above the average; and when he entered on his senior year, and began sermonizing, he discouraged his teacher by the apparent lack of definite thought in his "plans." This was specially true when he was about to prepare a written sermon for criticism, and presented a plan on Exod. xvii. 5, 6: "And the Lord said unto Moses, Go on before the people, and take with thee of the elders of Israel; and thy rod, wherewith thou smotest the river, take in thine hand, and go. Behold, I will stand before thee there upon the rock in Horeb; and thou shalt smite the rock, and there shall come water out of it that the people may drink."

In vain did I endeavor to gather from his "plan" what he purposed to do with this striking text, and at last frankly told him I feared he would "make nothing of it" in writing, unless he succeeded better in putting on paper the ideas which he proposed to amplify. Confident, however, that he could say at length what he could not in brief, he went to work, and in due time presented himself before his critics, his teacher and fellow-students, with a sermon in which he set forth in a clear, striking, forcible style, the work of the ministry, that of guiding and feeding the flock, under three heads: (1) Man's part, "Go thou, take the rod, smite the rock;" (2) God's part, "I will stand before thee upon the rock; and (3) the result, — "There shall come water out of it."

"This result is sure to follow when the antecedent conditions have been complied with; and, if it follow not, either God is false to his promise, or we to our duty. Mere *going* is not enough; nor is it sufficient to take the rod: we must *smite*, and when and where God bids us.

"How solemn the responsibility of standing thus, with God before us, ready to bless or curse, according as we do, or fail to do, as he has bidden us!" As he went on, opening up and enforcing these ideas, one by one the critics' pencils dropped from their hands; and when, at last, he dwelt upon the awful guilt of the unsuccessful minister, and the blessedness of the privilege of being, with God's help, a successful one, opening fountains of living water for thirsty, perishing souls, tears stood in all eyes. Teacher and pupils alike felt that we were in the presence of God, and, instead of criticising the preacher, needed to look to our own case.

And when, at length, the usual criticisms were called for, "It is a good sermon: let us pray," was the only response.

Criticism had been disarmed in the most effectual way, by making all feel that God was in that place, ready to bring us all into judgment.

VI.

LITTLE GREGORY.

NEARLY twenty years ago Mr. Dunmore, then a missionary at Diarberkir, a city on the Tigris, spent a night at Harpoot.

The news soon reached the market-place, and spread from shop to shop; for in those days a Frank was a new wonder in this city. The people soon learned that the stranger was a "missionary," one of the "wolves in sheep's clothing" that had, "in these latter days," begun to prowl about the Christian folds. The pious and vigilant gave an ominous shake of the head, made the sign of the cross oftener, and passed their beads through their fingers with greater rapidity, an evidence that they were fully aware of approaching danger.

Doubtless the shepherds warned their flocks, and commanded that all precautions should be taken, weak places strengthened, and the feeble ones helped out of danger's reach. Fathers carried the news to their homes, and kept strict watch there, lest some of their grown sons should be found outside after nightfall, and thus become a prey to the dreaded foe. Mothers listened with hushed voices, and pressed their little ones to their bosoms, lest some baleful influence should reach them even within their home-circles. The grandmothers, too, were all at church next morning, and forgot their gossip and match-making during the service, while, with unusual devoutness, they made the sign of the cross on their breasts, and many genuflexions of bending, bowing, kneeling, and kissing the floor, which is their *yergur-bakootune* (earth-kissing); or, as we should say, worship. They believed all they had heard about these "destroyers of the religion of their fathers." This man was a real specimen of the "infidel Protes." He would have great influence over all who ventured near him. If even one should touch his books, or drink *sherbet*[1] with him, he would become dazed, and an apostate from the religion of his ancestors.

In spite of all these precautions, a few sought out the stranger, and among them a little tailor, who was from a neighboring village. Was it because he had no father or mother near to watch over him? We know not; but we do know that he will bless God throughout eternity for what he obtained from the despised missionary. He did not rush forward, and demand that the missionary prove his new doctrines. No: he was a

[1] A sweet drink.

timid, shrinking youth, and listened in silence. When those who had come in left, he politely asked for a Testament, and, paying for and putting it in his bosom, went out.

Thus one little seed was sown that was to take root in good ground, and bring forth much fruit.

I feel very sure that you will all be interested to watch it, and see how God watered it, till it burst forth into such a beautiful, comely tree, that others sought to rest under its shadow. A few years passed; and we find this same young tailor, with several others, gathered into a class in Harpoot, and receiving daily instruction from the missionaries, who are now not mere sojourners, but permanently settled here. You will notice him at once; for his face is radiant and earnest, and his bearing polite. But you will see he is the same diffident young man that we met at the room of the missionary. A lady enters the room. Oriental politeness does not require him to rise, unless she is an aged lady; but at once he is on his feet, and needs not to be told that Occidental politeness requires it; for his politeness is "love manifested in a loving manner." In 1859 a school for preparing young men for the ministry was opened at Harpoot; and the "little tailor," whom we henceforth called Little Krekore (Gregory), entered with seventeen others. Among this first class were some of greater ability as scholars, but none that seemed to come so near to the likeness of the "beloved apostle." He graduated with honor, yes, more, with the love of *all* his classmates; which is as rare a thing in the East as in the West.

He was immediately called to labor in Ichmeh, a large village about twenty miles east from Harpoot.

He had spent one of his winter vacations

there while in the seminary; and the people were *all* in love with him. Many who would not receive his new doctrines were pleased with his kind, polite, Christian bearing. A prominent lady was induced by her son, who had become a Protestant, to attend one of his evening meetings. She was unwilling to offend her brother-in-law, who opposed this new faith: so she crept along under a high wall that separated his shop from the street that led to the little Protestant chapel, and thus entered for the first time; but it was not to be the last. Like the "little tailor," she heard things there that touched her heart, if they did not daze her brain; and "I couldn't stay away," was her answer when asked why she went. The little Primer became from that day her daily companion. It could be found on her table when she kneaded the bread, or under the cushion near her wheel. She was ever ready now for her lesson when her elder son came in from his work, or a younger one came from school.

Soon this whole house, of some fifty souls, was won over to "Krekore's side," and was an acquisition worth having. Some of its members were to be real pillars in Christ's church here; and Hach Hatoon (Lady Cross), who was the first to learn to read among the women, was to be a real "mother in Israel." Soon one of the priests of the village became uneasy. Secretly he bought a Bible; and after his children were all sleeping for the night, and the outer door bolted, he drew it forth from its hiding-place, and read to his wife some of its, to them, new truths. "We read and wept together," said the wife; "and the more we read, the sweeter it grew, and the wider our eyes were opened. We looked on our sleeping children, and knew, that, if what we had been doing should be known, we should soon be without the bread to fill their mouths. We carefully concealed the Bible: but night after night we continued our reading till we could endure it no longer; and I said to my husband, 'Emmanuel, we will act as the Bible tells us to, even if, hand in hand, we must beg our bread from door to door.'" They were shunned, persecuted, snowballed, and cursed; but, with "Little Krekore" to strengthen them, they were firm. The time had now come to unite the disciples into a church; and the "beloved teacher," as they had hitherto called Krekore, was to be their pastor. The chapel was small; but it could be enlarged a little by removing a partition.

A joyful crowd gathered, and among them the missionary teachers, and the classmates of Krekore. He was the first one from the Harpoot seminary to be inducted into the office of the ministry. His chapel was a very mean building with mud walls; and his house was so small, that one of the missionaries gave it the undignified name of "mousehole." We never knew him to falter but once; and then the missionaries voted to ask his people to take more of his salary upon themselves. He felt that they would not. His wife was an invalid; and he lacked almost every thing that makes home comfortable. The people had not then learned to give, or to think of their pastor's wants, as they now do. Washing-day found no tubs; and once Krekore, coming in, found his wife in tears. Like some other ministers' wives, she did not always find it so pleasant to borrow, even though everybody was pleased with the minister. He said, "Martha, don't weep. If God sees it best for us to have these things, he will surely send them." Not many days after, a brother came from Harpoot, bringing just the needed vessels,— a copper boiler and tub. Pastor Krekore met this brother in the street, and came back with quick steps to his house, saying, "Look here, Martha: did I not tell you these would come in God's time?"

He felt the need of some books; but how should he get them? They would cost two or three months' salary; and he could ill afford so much at once. He thought it all over, and then went to a brother, and asked if he could lend him the money, and receive his pay in small sums. "You can only live on your salary now; and how can you save for the books? Here, take this, and get the books you need." The twenty dollars were soon in the hand of the missionary, and the books ordered.

He was not content with the office of pastor, but, like a faithful shepherd, knew all about his sheep. Even the lambs were not afraid of him.

He taught the women, old and young, to read, and opened a weekly meeting for them; for his wife was too much an invalid to help him in this. He was so kind to his wife, that the women said he must be a good man; and thus he won them over to his Master and theirs. And some came to care for the invalid wife who would not speak to her or answer a question. One woman said, "I used to fill my ears with cotton, so that I could not hear what you said, I was so afraid you would make a Prote of me; but I could not see you suffer, and that kind little man wait on you alone." But a better day was dawning for him who could always trust in God, and wait his time. The old chapel was full to overflowing, and the people felt that they must " arise and build ; " and, with some help from the missionaries, they built a large, commodious church, very plain, but, when finished, as good as is needed. The "mouse-hole," too, has given place to a nice house of five rooms, and a nice court.

Many things are still needed to make this house all that we can wish for this good man and wife; but God will send them all in his own good time. The people are independent, and hard to manage; but God raised up this patient, polite, loving Christian man for this place. The church and community are both growing; and we can see no reason why all of the nominally Christian inhabitants of Ichmeh should not become Protestants from the influence of this young man. Would that the lone missionary who sold him the Testament could come and see the results with his own eyes! But he has been called to a higher service, and perhaps will receive the joyful news from Pastor Krekore himself, when they meet in some one of the "many mansions" in our Father's house.

VII.

SEED BY THE WAYSIDE.

NOT spiritually did it thus *fall*, to be devoured by fowls of the air; but literally, and with intent, was it thus cast, and it sprung up, and yielded a rich harvest. In 1860, when the village of Ichmeh was first occupied as a missionary out-station, a person passing through the village on horseback called out to a company of men by the roadside, "A new missionary is going to preach in the Protestant chapel, go and hear him;" and passed on his way, to learn, years subsequently, the influence of that one word. One from among the crowd started for the chapel, when all broke forth in a storm of ridicule against " the man who was turning Prote." "I am not such, and don't propose to be," replied he. "But I *am* free to go where I please; and, as you try to prevent me, I shall surely go and hear that man preach."

He went, and continued to go, never again going to the Armenian Church. And he not only became a Protestant, but a sincere Christian, and a pillar in the church. Of his three sons, the eldest, Bedros, had become a Protestant before his father, and borne bitter persecution from him. They all became Christians; and two of them, preachers, graduating at Harpoot Theological Seminary. Bedros ("Peter") did not, while in the seminary, excite very brilliant hopes for his future. His success as a student was below the average; and, when he began to preach written sermons for criticism, we came near feeling that we had lost our labor, that his efforts would not repay the interest of the money invested in educating him. By some who esteemed themselves, and were esteemed by us, hopeful candidates, we were blamed for bringing reproach on the seminary by retaining such men in it. But, while he failed to write sermons fit to criticise (the very idea of criticism seeming to frighten away his clear, connected thoughts, if he had any), he had two redeeming traits, which induced us to be patient to the end, and allow him to graduate. He had spent his winter vacations in Aghansi, a village upon Harpoot plain, in which a hopeful spiritual work had opened.

These two traits — plain, homely commonsense, enabling him to adapt himself to all classes of persons, and a burning zeal to lead men to Christ — had won at once the hearts of many of the simple-minded people; and we felt that such a man should not, because of a little dullness in the class-room, be dismissed to his saw, hammer, and planes. The result justified our decision. Called at graduation to go with his wife, a kindred spirit, to a hard district of our mission-field, he at once joyfully accepted; his only regret being, that he could not continue the good work begun in Aghansi, where the people, who, but a short time before, had in vain striven to drive him from their town, now even more earnestly desired his coming, pledging a part of his support from the first.

Located in Horhor, an Armenian town in the midst of the Koordish mountains, some eighty miles north-east from Harpoot, he had about him, within a radius of thirty miles, a large and almost totally benighted population of Armenians and Koords, among whom, for the space of a little less than four years, he labored with the zeal of a Paul, seeking by all means to win some to Christ. And it was a peculiarity of his labors, that, while they did not result in large accessions to the nominally Protestant ranks, most who were won were won to Christ. His was a weeping, as well as earnest, ministry. He spent hours in praying and weeping over special cases of persons whom he felt that he must see in the kingdom.

One " thorn," for the removal of which he besought the Lord more than thrice, were two brothers in Horhor, the only nominal adherents of the gospel at his arrival there, but who he felt, and felt truly, were mere Protestants, not Christians. *They* felt that they were safe, and were loud mouthed in proclaiming the excellences of the new system; while, by their worldly-mindedness, covetousness, and dislike of Bedros' plain, searching preaching, they proclaimed themselves strangers to the power of the gospel. Never did we visit him in his mountain home, without bringing away cheer from some story of the hopeful conversion of some one for whom he had been praying and laboring. It was his pleasure to guide "old Sarah" of Temran to Christ, after she had been intellectually won to the truth. Among others in Horhor for whose conversion he labored and prayed specially was an aged man. At last the poor old man was taken suddenly ill, and at midnight sent for Bedros, who, going at once, found him dead, with his Testament opened, and marked at the text, "Come unto me, all ye that labor and are heavy laden, and I will give you rest." His converts caught something of his spirit; and we hear of one of them, who, having labored to lead a fellow-traveler to the truth, at length knelt and prayed with him by the roadside, and at rising threw his arms about him, exclaiming, "Oh, I do so much wish to see you a Christian!"

He won throughout all the district the

name of being a saint; and many who profess to hate Protestantism bear witness that there was one Christian among them. "Bedros," say they, "was a truly good man. He was what he professed to be." He was specially careful to consecrate a portion of his earnings to the Lord's treasury, and from his salary of ninety-six dollars per annum, he, with a family of seven to support, paid tithes for Christian work; though we may as well acknowledge, that, when his tithes fell into our hands, we indirectly turned them back into the treasury of the giver, as the man engaged in the *most Christian work* we could find, and most in need of the money. Of his four sons, too, he consecrated the two brightest to the special service of Christ in his ministry, saying, "He shall have the best." In like manner, his first-born daughter was specially set apart for "Christ to use in some way in his ministry." These three, he felt, must have a good education to fit them for their work; and he trained them as if he expected the consecration to be accepted.

And he not only taught, but lived, the gospel before them. He always seemed full of Christ and his precious work, loving to talk of nothing else. He, with more right than any one else among our Christian laborers, might have uttered the sentiments of the hymn, —

> "My Jesus shall still be my theme
> While on this earth I stay:
> I'll sing my Jesus' lovely name,
> When all things else decay.
>
> When I appear in yonder cloud,
> With all his favored throng,
> Then will I sing more sweet, more loud;
> And Christ shall be my song."

And such, we doubt not, he is now. The Master at length removed the "thorn;" and in Bedros' last letter to us, dated July, 1873, he tells his joy in the hopeful conversion and happy death of one of the two "Protestants" of Horhor, and the changed appearance of the other, and of the happy death of one of his sabbath-school scholars.

Shortly after, he made a missionary visit to Hopoos, a hostile town in which we have for years vainly tried to locate a preacher. Whether he there had unusual excitement and hardship, we know not; but he returned with fever upon him, which at once assumed the typhus form, and ended his life in a week. He at the first told his wife he should die, and was happy in the thought of going, and assured her that the widow's and orphan's God would care for her and the little ones; and to him he commended them. There was little time for dying testimony; for the dread fever speedily asserted its full power; and happily there was no need of it.

His had been an unmistakable life-witness. And, while he lay upon his death-bed in Horhor, his father was, in like manner, prostrated in Ichmeh, having, like the son, though in a different style, borne testimony to the power of the gospel. Neither, probably, knew here of the other's illness, which they first learned from each other's lips in that world where "there shall be no more death, neither sorrow nor crying, neither shall there be any more pain; for the former things are passed away."

"Who shall weep when the righteous die?
Who shall mourn when the good depart?
When the soul of the godly away shall fly,
Who shall lay the loss to heart?"

"He has gone in peace; he has laid him down
To sleep till the dawn of a brighter day;
And he shall wake on that holy morn,
When sorrow and sighing shall flee away."

VIII.

DEACON HAGOP.

IN the Orient 'tis sometimes hard to tell by which of his many names to call a man, who, like our deacon Hagop ("Jacob"), is an immigrant, has a trade, and happens to have seen Jerusalem, and won the title of Mahdesi ("seer of the death"), or its equivalent Turkish, Haji ("pilgrim"). Thus the deacon was known as Mahdesi and Haji Hagop, Hagop of Maden, (the place from which he emigrated to Harpoot), Saätji ("watchmaker") Hagop, Haji Agha ("pilgrim, esquire"), a name given by his friends to any one, Armenian or Turk, who has seen Jerusalem or Mecca, and lastly, in old age, as Deacon Hagop, and Haji Baba ("pilgrim father"), the latter a pet name given him by the Protestant community.

The most singular fact in regard to this medley of names is, that none of them was the true one, which would have been, in real Scripture style, Hagop, *son* of — his father, or grand, or some great-grand sire, according to the taste of himself or parents. Here we get an inlook into the biblical style of calling persons by different names.

The time of our hero's birth let some Yankee "guess" (we forgot to ask him to do it in time); the place, some town of the mountainous district lying between the two branches of the Euphrates, to the north of Harpoot.

Those who, half a century ago, were ferried over into this region of hopeless oppression, to remain there, might well recall Dante's awful inscription over the entrance of his Inferno; for, with its pitiless oppression, its cruelties and hopeless miseries, it was indeed a

> "Region of sorrow, doleful shades, where peace
> And rest could never dwell, hope never came,
> That comes to all."

The Mohammedan owners of the soil, haughty despisers and fanatical haters of the Christian ryots, whose ancestry had been conquered and despoiled by the Moslem invaders, would neither suffer them to emigrate, nor to enjoy at home any of the rights of manhood. The present inhabitants tell of the time, not yet wholly past in the darker corners of the district, when they imagined they had been born only to be tied up by the hands, and beaten at the bidding of their oppressors; and I have myself seen the bruised and blackened body of a poor victim who had died under blows thus inflicted by a fellow Christian, at the bidding of their Turkish master, for a slight offense.

From this region, while little Hagop was yet an infant, his parents, leaving all behind, escaped to Maden, then the capital of the Harpoot district. His own memory did not reach back to those days of fear and flight; but some modern scenes on the same road aid us in vividly picturing the anxiety and alarm of the fleeing family, especially as they neared the ferry, where, to this day, families not evidently under powerful protection are obliged to pay illegal and exorbitant toll to the ferrymen for the privilege of escape from this land of bondage.

The penalty of failure to satisfy this rapacity would have been betrayal into the hands of their pursuers. Nor, in escaping to the capital town, had they escaped from scenes of oppression and bloodshed. At least, so thought young Jacob, when, day after day, he saw the bloody cimeter sever the heads of victims innocent or guilty, according as the whim took the pasha and his brother rulers, till the work of blood reached a climax in a rebellion, and the rolling of some threescore and ten heads down the Euphrates' banks together, — whether for real rebellion, or to inspire fear among supposed would-be rebels, is uncertain. This, however, was the end of Maden's day as capital, the chief vestiges of whose former glory are now scores of roofless houses, and a still greater number of pretentious tombs of big Turks of the olden time, few if any of whose posterity remain; for the centralization of the rebellion in Harpoot, under the leadership of a pasha's widow, led the ruling pasha hither with his army, where he felt compelled to remain, thus making this city — or rather the village of Mezereh, three miles to the south — the new capital of the district, and leaving Maden to sink to its present obscurity.

We know not whether any of Hagop's relatives survived to accompany him and the emigrating multitude who came to gather about the rulers, and feed upon government crumbs in and about the new capital. Suffice it to say, none remain; nor have any been seen since the days of missionary occupation, beginning about twenty years ago. Here Mr. Dunmore, the first missionary, found him, a man of some threescore years, and soon had the joy of welcoming him to the circle of gospel believers, — a joy which, to the day of his death, the convert increased by a steadfast adhesion to the truth, and an ever increasing clearness of Christian experience.

And there was room for growth; for though a saint, he was not at first, even if he subsequently became, a perfect one. One sadly prominent stain, which was only washed away by his being providentially made to pass through deep waters of affliction in the line of his sin, was that of niggardliness. Never can the writer forget the stingy positiveness with which, though then in receipt of an ample salary from the missionary treasury, as bookseller, he protested his utter inability to pay more than six cents a month towards the salary of the pastor they were about to settle. But we shall see, in due time, how all this was changed, and he made meet for that world into which no sordid soul shall ever enter. Like most men of his class, he was extremely narrow minded; and like too many, who, though saved by grace, fail to secure a generous, broad, intelligent Christian culture, he remained to the last a man of somewhat narrow views. Thank God, we shall all have plenty of room, time, and means for the largest growth up there, where years ago our old pilgrim began effectively his work of large development.

It hardly need be said, that, like all the rest of his people in those days, he was very ignorant. But this lack of book-culture perhaps aided, rather than hindered, the development of a native shrewdness which often stood him in good stead in time of need.

Of this he gave a good specimen when once a government defaulter, who denied his debt, was brought for trial before the court of which he was a member. As, in the absence of proof to fix the debt upon him, the man was about to take the customary oath, denying it, Hagop requested that the case be left to him. Then — saying to the man, "I am about to swear you on this Book of God, and if, with your hand on this, you tell a lie, neither can the priest pardon you in this world, nor will God in the next; for you will be guilty of blasphemy against the Holy Ghost, and will be for ever lost " — he bade him place his hand on the volume, and said, "Tell me, do you owe this money, or not?"—"I do," said the frightened debtor; and the government got its dues. Would that some such new and effective form of oath might be discovered for defaulters elsewhere! Two Oriental notions were firmly fixed in his mind,—one, that the wife should implicitly obey her husband in all things; and, second, that, on the death of one wife, the afflicted husband should make haste to honor her memory, and console his grief, by taking another.

Unfortunately, his first wife, who was a model of obedience, died, and, to our surprise, late one evening, a few days after her death, he came in, and in a hasty, excited way, said to Mr. Dunmore, "I have found a woman. Come at once and marry me."

But alas! "Marry in haste, and repent at leisure," had an illustration in his case; for the woman so hastily chosen proved to be more of a means of grace than a saint, and sorely tried the good old man's patience.

"Ah!" said he sadly one day, "why is it that all missionaries' wives are angels? Mine is very disobedient. Do come over, and exhort her to obey me." But, fearing that our Socrates was probably not a faultless husband, we declined to exhort his Xantippe; and to the day of his death she helped him to grow in the grace of patience.

Against his continuing in his business as bookseller for the missionaries, there were two valid objections, — one, his utter inability to be convinced of the reasonableness of the rule requiring payment in full for books at time of sale. This inability was, however, removed by another rule overpowering a weaker part of his nature, according to which he paid for all books sold. He lost about two dollars in this way, and then learned, that, by trying, he could say "No" to an importunate, impecunious purchaser.

GRACE ILLUSTRATED. 109

A second and insurmountable objection was the feeling of the new missionaries, that bookselling should not be confined to one or any limited number of salaried men, nor to such "spiritual loafing and smoking shops," as observation showed the tendency of Oriental bookshops to be, but that all who professed to love the Bible should personally and gratuitously aid in selling it. It is the resolute carrying-out of this principle which has resulted in scattering so many thousands of good books in this mission-field,[1] and produced outside the very mistaken impression, that, in Harpoot, people are so hungry for the Word, that Bibles "sell themselves." Sore

---

[1] The following books have been sold from the Harpoot book depository during the past seventeen years:—

Bibles in different languages	4,250
Portions of Scripture in different languages	20,000
Other religious volumes	39,233
School-books	23,816
Total	87,899

was the affliction of the poor bookseller, as, by the force of this new idea, he saw rivals rising up to take away his trade; and when, at length, his monthly sales were reduced to less than a dollar, and he got the courage to protest against the "new notion," which threatened to deprive him at once of both his bread, and his joy in selling *the Book*, we, too, took courage to say, "You see that the work can be more cheaply and effectively done in this way," and to propose to him to give up his bookshop cushion, and go into *active* service.

In this he was employed chiefly as a traveling evangelist, proving himself earnest and efficient, going on horseback from place to place, till, in 1861, he with his horse fell over an embankment, causing such injuries as unfitted him for active service; and as failing eyesight prevented his return to his early trade of repairing watches, and we could not again employ him in bookselling, he was without visible means of support. In vain did we secure a supply of "Yankee notions" in Oriental demand, hoping, that, by the profits on their sale, the good old man might earn his bread.

"Yankee notions" are one thing in the hands of a Yankee, and another and very different thing in those of an unpractical Oriental like Deacon Hagop. The result was, that what "notions" he didn't eat were sold at cost; and selling his house, and removing to a cheaper one, he decided to "wait upon the Lord." This he did with the simple, clinging faith of a little child. In vain did his old friends gather about him, saying, "See how these missionaries treat you in your old age! Come back to the Armenian Church, and we will support you."

His uniform reply was, "I have put my trust in the Lord; and, though he slay me, I will continue to trust in him. But I do not believe he will forsake me." We all commended his case to Him who inspired the utterance, "I have been young, and now am old, yet have I not seen the righteous forsaken, nor his seed begging bread." And who can say that the result was not a direct and striking answer to prayer?

A letter by Mr. Barnum, giving some facts of the case, found its way to an English magazine, a copy of which, in like manner, "found its way" into the hands of an English-speaking Dutchman on the continent of Europe, whose sympathies were so moved, that he at once collected quite a sum of money, a bank-check for which he inclosed to Mr. Barnum, addressing the letter to him at Harpoot. On reaching Turkey, its English direction was, of course, useless; and the postmasters sent it hither and thither in search of a foreign claimant. The annual meeting of the Mission to Eastern Turkey, with which Harpoot is connected, being in session in Bitlis, distant from Harpoot about ten days direct, but about a month by post (!) Mr. Barnum had just presented the case of Hagop for consultation, when the post arrived with the letter and money in search of the long-sought claimant. One sentence of its quaint English was, "If the Lord Jesus *thinks well of it*, I desire thus to support Hagop as long as he shall live." We feared to tell the aged pilgrim this promise, lest he should be overmuch tempted to put his trust in man. He knew that He in whom he trusted sent him some eight dollars month by month; and he believed that he would do it to the last. He loved his human benefactor, and wrote him letters, which we translated and forwarded; and the promise to support him, if Jesus thought well of it, was made good. Of the last remittance, only enough was left to pay the expense of his funeral, and place a plain granite stone to mark his grave. Much to our disappointment, though we subsequently repeatedly wrote to our Dutch friend, no response has come.

It was during these years of patient waiting and trusting, that the fruits of grace abounded, to the continually increasing exclusion of nature's weeds. He who, in the time of prosperity, had grudgingly pledged six cents a month for Christ's cause, now, in sickness and poverty, when living by faith, gladly, and unsolicited, gave many times the amount.

Then he seemed to *feel* what before he had only *said*, that he and all his belonged to Christ; and his niggardliness was all gone. In his soul, expanded, illumined, and purified by divine grace, it could find no corner dark and foul enough to hide its execrable shape. The nearer he felt the end of his earthly labors to be, the dearer to him were those for whom he had labored.

Not long before his last illness, feeling that he had strength for such a journey, if taken slowly, he said, " I must go again, and visit my brethren in every city where I have preached the word of the Lord, and see how they do." Extending his tour beyond the bounds of our own field, he visited Bitlis and Erzroom, confirming the brethren, being received by all with that respect and affection which his venerable appearance, and Saint-John-like Christian character and exhortations, were fitted to secure. Returning, he felt that his earthly service was nearly ended, and not long afterwards retired to his sick-room, to wait, a patient sufferer, for the hour of his release.

" The chamber where the good man meets his fate
  Is privileged above the common walks of life; "

and so pre-eminently was his.

Among this people, all means, honest and dishonest, are resorted to, to conceal from a dying man the fact of death's approach, lest his terror and distress hasten the hour of his departure. And such is the popular dread of all of death's surroundings, that the body of one who dies too late in the day for the usual hurried burial must be at least hastily wrapped in the customary shroud, and hurried off to the church, to be ready for the early morning burial. But here was one, who, to all his old companions (who came in numbers to see him), not only predicted his speedy departure, but assured them that he was joyful in the thought of going. In the intervals between his asthmatic sufferings, he tried to point them to Him whose grace had thus removed the fear and dread of death, and exhorted them to secure him as a friend for their own coming time of need.

Besides himself, but one in that white-bearded company — "the aged auctioneer" — had been united with the little company of gospel believers; and those death-bed exhortations, even, seemed to make but little permanent impression. Some thought him beside himself; others listened in incredulous amazement; while others felt and wept, and went away, and forgot it all. They came, indeed, as he had requested, and sat around his coffin on his burial day, and wept again, as we sung the hymn he had selected, —

> "Come sing to me of heaven
> When I'm about to die:
> Sing songs of holy ecstasy,
> To waft my soul on high.
> There'll be no sorrow there,
> There'll be no sorrow there:
> In heaven above, where all is love,
> There'll be no sorrow there!"

But to this hour, those yet alive, whose tears

then fell fastest, are apparently most stony-hearted, and least likely to follow him up the shining way. So true it is, that for the Ethiopian to change his skin, and the leopard his spots, is impossible with men, possible only to Him whose word can raise the dead, and who saves from the company of white-haired rebels only enough to illustrate and verify the reality and power of his almighty grace.

Such was the nature of his disease as to compel him to spend day and night in a sitting posture, and that often in the keenest torture. After his paroxysms of distress, he would point up, and say, "There is no coughing up there; no coughing up there!" "I am going to a wedding, to the marriage-supper of the Lamb," were the last words the writer heard him utter; and soon he did join the company of the redeemed, continuing to the last patient, peaceful, full of joy.

A weeping company bore his remains to the grave which he had dug beside that of his wife, and placed over it the gray granite block he had prepared to mark the spot.

The Word was read, a hymn sung, and prayer made, and we left him to wait the resurrection morn, feeling, as we came away, that the Master scatters such life and death scenes here and there along our pathway, to prevent our weak faith from failing in the hard, ungrateful work we have to do. It was said above, that the good man loved his Dutch benefactor. To some, this statement may seem so necessarily true as to be unnecessary, and still more uncalled for the statement, that, to the last, he was grateful to those who had made him acquainted with the gospel; not merely to that always admired benefactor, "the Board," around which gathers the halo of ethereal, distant beneficence, but also to its seen, human representatives, the missionaries, with their many real, and more imagined, imperfections.

We devoutly hope that the experience of missionaries to *real heathen* may be different from that of most who labor for " nominal Christians;" but that those who, if hungry, would be grateful to any passer-by who should give them a piece of bread, or a bowl of soup, are frequently increasingly ungrateful to those who have brought them the bread and the water of life, is a fact explainable by no philosophy but that of the perverse inconsistency of poor human nature. Are we to suppose that missionaries, instead of remaining to labor for the permanent planting of Christian institutions, should simply proclaim the gospel, and pass along, not waiting for the ingratitude and abuse of those apparently most blessed (!) by it? It would sometimes seem that gratitude, called by some one a "plant of slow growth," seldom finds room and soil for growing in the newly enlightened adult soul in this world. Be that as it may, the heart of the missionary in this land is oftener saddened by reproachful demands for unreceived benefits than cheered by grateful acknowledgment of those bestowed. And those proposing to enter upon the work may as well be forewarned. But let them, also, be fore-armed by the assurance that here and there some life or death scene will be so radiant with the luster of divine grace as to cause to be forgotten all the gloom and sadness which follow even the most trying exhibitions of human imperfection and sin.

In the missionary scale, the enjoyment of one growing, grateful saint, outweighs the trial of a score of complaining ones; and the Master, if we trust his promise, will take care, that, in addition to his own blessed presence, the supply of visible, tangible cheer, shall abound to those who need it — as who of us does not at times?

IX.

THE BROKEN VOW.

SOME twelve years ago, a copy of the New Testament, in the modern tongue, found its way into the hands of a tailor, a "reader" in one of the Armenian churches in Harpoot, and stirred within him new and strange thoughts,—questionings concerning his own religious experience and that of those about him. These questions he used to commit to writing for further thought and examination; and once, when a missionary called at his home, the question-paper was brought out to aid in seeking the light he needed. Finding two other young men, who, with him, felt an interest in studying the new book, they three became especially earnest in the worship of their church, being desirous even of having the people leave, and close the church-doors upon them, that they might have longer space for united worship.

These companions both died; one apparently being prepared for death, leaving the young tailor still feeling his way toward full gospel light and liberty.

A Protestant meeting being opened in his ward of the city, he, after many questionings, concluded to go for once. To his surprise, he found that these innovators talked well and truly, raising just the questions which had been troubling him, and professing to answer them. He was so troubled by this, and alarmed, lest they should steal his affections from his own church, that he went, and, kneeling before the altar, made a solemn vow never to separate from her communion. Having thus fortified his resolutions, and made his position safe from Protestant attack, he continued to attend their meetings, where, to his dismay, he found that even his oath-bound resolutions were like the vow of darkness to withstand mid-day light, or of a lump of ice to resist the noonday sun. He saw, that, to hold to his purpose, he must escape from the light and heat which radiated from the open Bible on the Protestant pulpit.

Again he knelt before the altar with the feeling, "I must be on one side or the other. Which shall it be? Did I do right in making that vow? and is it binding upon me?" There, alone with his God, he settled the question in the negative. Not only was the vow not binding upon his conscience, but he had done wrong in making it. From that hour, he was a recognized adherent of the evangelical party, and, with his family, was always present at the meetings.

And not only so much, but saying to himself, "These services cost something, and I should pay my part towards them," he sought out the treasurer, and entered his name among the subscribers for the pastor's salary. With such principles, and such a beginning, it is not strange that he was speedily known as a leading member of the church, nor that, when a successor was needed for "Deacon Hagop," hands were laid upon the head of Kincose, and that he has been, and still is, one of the chief pillars of the church.

X.

ONE OF GOD'S HIDDEN ONES.

BY MISS HATTIE SEYMOUR.

J—— entered the female seminary, we can not say definitely at what age; though, when asked how old she was, she replied, "Sixty." Her teacher laughed, and told her that was impossible. "Well," said J——, "perhaps I am fifty." As she only *guessed* at her age, we may be allowed to do the same; and probably a more correct estimate would be, that forty summers had passed over her head. She is a woman of gentle spirit, kind in feeling and manner.

She did not know her letters when she entered school; and to learn to read at her age seemed a most formidable undertaking.

She began *aip, pen, kiva* (a, b, c) with a good will; but as day after day passed, and, notwithstanding her hard work over her lessons, she did not make much progress, she said to her teacher, "I can never learn to read. My mind has never been worked, and my brain is thick. I study away at the first letter till I think I have learned it, and then try the second; but, when I turn back to the first, I have forgotten its name."

As day after day, sad and discouraged, she repeated her conviction to her teacher, that she should never learn to read, she was advised to try this plan, — never to open her book to study, without first silently lifting her heart in prayer, that her mind might be quickened, and that God would send down special grace to help her remember. The answer to her prayers seemed almost a miracle. 'Tis faith that

"Laughs at impossibilities,
And cries, 'It shall be done.'"

And simple faith and prayer brought a daily supply of strength to poor J——, which carried her triumphantly through the primer her first year in school. It was pleasant to see her happy face as she entered the second year, bearing her New Testament reverently in her hands. Her reading was not now a mere lesson to her. She sat one day in the class with several other women, one of whom read Matthew's account of our Lord's crucifixion. There was some familiar talk about the "old, old story;" and then J—— was called, in her turn, to read. She rose slowly, and, with averted face, took her seat by her teacher, but, instead of reading, bowed her face in her hands, and was evidently trying to suppress her sobs. "Why, J——," her teacher asked in surprise, "what is the matter?"—"I can never hear that story of Christ's death," she said, "without crying." Happy J——!

Well might one, who, from a child, had known the Holy Scriptures, envy you the freshness and tenderness of your feelings, and feel that the teacher should sit at the pupil's feet, and learn of him.

The day of fasting and prayer, just after the opening of J——'s second year in school, was one of tender interest. Those present in the morning prayer-meeting will not soon forget J——'s face, working with deep emotion, as she said with tremulous voice, "I want you all to pray for me. I am weak; I don't know any thing; I am very bad; but I want to be a Christian." Later in the day, her deep contrition had another element mingled with it; and the burden of her heart and words seemed to be,—

"I'm a poor sinner, and nothing at all;
But Jesus Christ is my all in all."

And afterwards, whenever inquiry was

made as to whether she still loved and trusted Christ, she answered with the simplicity of a child, that she was sure she did. "And why are you so sure?" she was once asked. "Because," she said, laying her hand upon her heart, "I feel such a warmth here whenever I think of him." "Blessed are the meek and single-hearted," says Thomas À Kempis; "for they shall possess the abundance of peace."

XI.

THE LITTLE HUMPBACK.

NEAR the city of Arabkir, nestled among the Anti-Taurus Mountains, is the wretched little village of Shèpik. Poverty seems written over every door; but this is the place where blind John Concordance first preached his "Tithe Sermon," which so aroused the poor, simple-minded Protestants of the village, that each male with willing heart consecrated the tenth of all his gains to the Lord's service. The influence of this sermon could not be shut up here; but the blind preacher was invited to preach it in other places, and many were convinced by his strong arguments that they had been robbing the Master's treasury.

More than twenty years before this revival of giving the "Lord's tenth" in Shèpik, a little girl was born in one of these humble homes. Her parents gave her the beautiful name, Kohar ("Jewel"). I know not why they gave her this name; for when she grew up she was neither handsome in features, nor comely in form, for she was humpbacked. This deformity may have been caused by some injury in her childhood; but the particulars we know not. We first hear of Kohar as the "bright little humpback," who had run away from her Shèpik home to Arabkir, to see the missionaries; or, rather, had tried to do so.

She heard in her village that some "Inglese" had come to Arabkir, a city only six miles away.

The neighbors came in to talk about these men with a "new religion," who "kept no fasts," and never "kissed the earth" in their worshiping. The priests shook their heads, and warned their flocks to beware of these "deceivers coming in these last days," these "wolves in sheep's clothing." Each new-comer from the city had some new thing to tell about the Protestants. "These people bring the Bible, and urge old and young to read it, even the women. They open schools, too, for both boys and girls. They give much honor to their wives, walking with them in the streets, and permitting them to enter a house first."

Little Kohar was greatly delighted with all these things; and she believed that such people could not be as wicked as her priest thought them to be. She was greatly troubled. Her priest was God's chosen servant. She had been baptized by him. He could read the holy Bible, and the books of the fathers; and he said these Protes were "bad, wicked men." But the others read the Bible too; and they have schools, and try to teach people to read the Bible for themselves.

The jewel covered up in the rubbish began to shine a little. This little girl longed for more knowledge. "Why should not she read the Bible for herself, and see what was written in that holy book sent down from God? These foreign women could read, and God had not struck them dead for their impiety; but they were trying to teach other women to read also." Her thirst for knowledge overcame all her fears; and she resolved to visit these strangers, and see for herself what kind of people they were.

Poor child! What can she do? She is only a girl, and can not go so far alone. Her parents would not consent to let her go, even if some one would take her to these people. She had never been taught to pray to Jesus to help her, and show her the right way; and would the "Blessed Virgin" help, when she wished to go to the very people who said it was wrong to pray to Mary? The desire filled her whole soul; and she forgot all her fears, forgot her weak back, and started to go alone to Arabkir. Her mother soon learned that she had run away, and hastened to the priest's house, and begged him to help her rescue her child. They went in pursuit, and soon overtook the poor girl, and led her back by her hair, that hung in long braids upon her shoulders. The missionary at Arabkir, hearing of this, visited Shèpik, and sought out Kohar. He was pleased with her earnestness, and felt that God was calling her to a higher service than the work in her poor village; but he told her she must not disobey her parents, and run away. "The Bible tells us to obey our parents. You must pray to the God of

KOHAR, (Little Humpback)

this holy Bible, Kohar; and he will hear you, and open a way for you to come to the school at Arabkir, where you can learn to read the Bible for yourself."

I have no doubt that she daily prayed for this one great desire of her heart; and God in heaven heard the little humpback's prayer; for the work in Arabkir prospered. Many were those who sought the new light, and were themselves enlightened, and went out to seek others, that they, too, might come and see, and believe for themselves. This light had entered the city; and, even though many had risen up against it, it could not be concealed under a bushel. The shining reached even to the mountain village, and was the topic of conversation in every house. Some, even of the wiser ones, bought the condemned Book, the "Prote Testament," and began to read for themselves about this "new faith." Then they told their neighbors, and compared this new book with the ancient one from which their priests read. "Why, brethren, these are just the same words; only one is in our ancient tongue, and the other in the modern. These people are right, and our priests are wrong. They are ignorant, and have kept us so." A desire for knowledge was awakened; but many shuddered at these new doctrines, and kept a more watchful lookout for their beloved ones.

The women especially felt that the religion that forbade them to call on the Holy Virgin was not to be tolerated. The Turk was bad enough; but these New Religionists were much more dangerous, especially to their children.

"I would rather my child should be a Turk than one of those Protes," was the language often heard from those calling themselves Christians.

The priest himself began to think about these strange doctrines, and read more carefully his smoky Bible, and to think less of his book of church forms and rules. The sabbath was discussed; and many began to say, "Surely the sabbath is holier than saints' days; but we profane God's day, while we carefully keep a great many saints' days."

Kohar's father and uncles began to talk of these things in the long winter evenings, when the neighbors would come in and tell of some new development in the neighboring city. The mother, too, listened, and seemed to be more softened towards her little girl, who would be drinking in all she heard, believing that God would soon send the answer to her earnest prayers, as the missionary had assured her he would.

These discussions were the wedge that God prepared to pry open the door to let his jewel come forth to the light of perfect day.

Kohar became a better child; and God was using her as a little preacher in her home, and thus softening her parents' hearts. They looked upon her crooked back, and pitied her; for she would never be married, and she could not work in the field, and thus aid her father. What can a village woman do, if too weak to labor with her husband, father, and brothers in the fields? The father and brothers would say, "Surely the housework is of very little account."

"How would it do to let those Inglese have Kohar?" was the thought that troubled father and mother. "Perhaps they, too, are Christians, and then our child will not be lost. By and by she will be only a burden to us; but, if we let her go to school, she may be able to help herself in some way. At any rate, they will care for her." It was a joyful day when she entered a Protestant family in Arabkir, and began to attend school. She made such progress, that, ere long, she was able to help the missionary's wife in the school, and finally became the teacher of the girls' school. She loved to study; and, when she heard that a seminary for girls was opened at Harpoot, she became uneasy even in her beloved work of teaching.

She was unwilling to sadden those who had done so much for her to fit her for this position; for she saw no one to take her place in the school. The desire grew, and became so strong, that she looked sad. The kind missionaries said, "Kohar, you are very much needed here; but in the spring you may go to Harpoot." The happy girl felt that God had answered her prayer a second time; and her heart was filled with joy and thanksgiving, and her face radiant with smiles. She was an earnest student, and, after her graduation, was selected as assistant in the seminary, where, for several years, she gave great satisfaction to the missionary teachers, and was beloved by all the girls, her Christian influence over whom filled the hearts of her superiors with joy, and they felt that their dear pupils were safe while they had such a constant example of earnest piety and patience to look up to. Kohar was at the head of the school-family; and seldom did her management need any interference, while she was ready to listen to any advice given her. During the long winter vacations, when the seminary was closed, and the girls sent home to teach, or aid their parents in the family, Kohar made long tours among the villages, sometimes spending several weeks in one place, teaching the women, holding prayer-meetings, and singing sweet songs, which the women often speak of as one of their pleasant recollections of her visits.

In this way she encouraged both the preachers and their wives, besides winning new sisters to the gospel.

She did not forget her native village nor her father, mother, and brothers. When visiting and talking, her fingers were busy making collars or edging, which she sold, and sent the avails to help support the pastor of Shèpik; for the light had not only entered her home, and enlightened her father and mother, and other members of the family, but now a church was formed; and the priest — who for years had burnt incense before the pictures of saints, and preached fast days and saints' days, — stood up to preach not the intercession of Mary, but that of Jesus the Son of man, as the only advocate between God and fallen man.

She remembered her parents in their poverty also, and often sent them something from her own earnings. Nor did she forget the foreign mission-work. Well do I remember the time when she gave five dollars to this work, while she had not clothing suitable for the cold winter before her. While seeking others' comfort, she forgot her own; and often her own health would have suffered from her unselfishness, had not some one cared for her. But He who cares even for the hungry ravens, and notes the sparrow's fall, put it into kind hearts to supply the warm garments needed for her frail body when she went out among the villages in midwinter. Her gratitude to the unseen givers, often far off in a (to her) strange land, was earnest and beautiful. It touched her tender heart to think that strangers should care for her, because they, too, loved the same Jesus she did; and she often spoke of the joy she should have in seeing these dear ones, and praising this same Jesus with them in heaven. During one of her vacations, she went to the city of Egin, where we had a preacher and his wife, but where the people looked with scorn upon Protestants. The women were superior to those of any other place in our mission-field, very neat and tidy in their dress and houses, but proud, and far away from the simple teachings of Jesus of Nazareth. She conversed with those who would lend a listening ear out of mere politeness. But soon some were ready to welcome her to their houses, though others hooted after her in the streets, crying out "Prote," even throwing stones at her. When the time came for her to return to Harpoot, she had won several women, who not only came to listen to her sweet words about Jesus, but were busy over their primer, learning to read, that they for themselves might study the sweet words of the Saviour about whom they had heard from Kohar. Among these pupils were women with white heads, patiently learning their *a, b, c's*. "You must not leave us," was the pleading cry of these women. "Who will care for us, if you go?" She urged that her presence was needed in the school; but they replied, "The missionaries can find some one else. Do not leave us now!"

She staid with them; but they were just as unwilling that she should leave them when the next spring came, and the next; and she has seen the work extend, till quite a strong Protestant community has grown up. Twenty-three persons, among them nine women, have joined a neighboring church, and are looking forward to the time when they can ordain their preacher, and become a separate church. Kohar has now a school of sixty pupils, and calls earnestly for an assistant; so that she may devote her time to those who are yet too proud to acknowledge that they need any good thing. Who of us could have foretold the success that has followed this poor little deformed girl, when we first saw her in her humble home among the mountains?

God has his jewels scattered all over the world; and he will cause them to shine when he has need of their light. He will call upon us to help him polish and refine them, if we are waiting to help him; and surely the reward will be glorious.

> "Sow in the morn thy seed;
>   At eve hold not thine hand;
> To doubt and fear give thou no heed;
>   Broadcast it o'er the land!
>
> Thou canst not toil in vain:
>   Cold, heat, and moist and dry
> Shall foster and mature the grain
>   For garners in the sky."

XII.

KOORDISH AMY.

SOME fifty miles north from Harpoot, the horizon is skirted by the towering range of the Anti-Taurus Mountains, which, stretching to the east, to Persia and the homes of the mountain Nestorians, and south-east, through Koordistan Proper, toward the Persian Gulf, are the home of untold numbers of Koordish tribes, whose ancestry, the *Carduchi*, held these same fastnesses nearly twenty-three hundred years ago, and near Redwan, one of the Koordish mission-stations of our native churches, disputed with Xenophon and his retreating "ten thousand" the passage through their land. Theories are various, curious, and some of them wild, in regard to the origin of this interesting people and their two languages,— the Koormanji and the Zaza Koordish. Suppose we "guess" that Nimrod, the "mighty hunter before the Lord," had two sons, who, with their companions, betook themselves to the mountains in search of game, and concluded to stay there, and replenish and hold their hunting-park. This supposition gives the old sportsman no mean posterity, since among the Koords are found some of the finest specimens of physical manhood in all the Orient.

If, however, commentators insist on a universal deluge, and the drowning out of all the children of Adam except those "eight souls," not even allowing Father Noah a few servants in the ark, let them provide progenitors for our Koords from among those eight, while we turn to our story.

About a score of years ago, in one of the districts near the city of Chemishgezek, one of this people, Murto by name, wedded a beautiful maiden named Bayzie. And, what was even more satisfactory than wedding a beauty (a thing which can not happen among the harem-owning Turks, with ugly black veils concealing their women's faces when abroad, nor even among the less exclusive Armenians), he, and all about him, knew that she was beautiful; for the Koords, while guarding with vindictive jealousy the virtue of their women, allow them to go and come with unveiled faces, a thing unknown among those about them.

And so it came to pass, that, when Murto and Bayzie had become the happy parents of two little girls, — Amy and Hedjie, — a wealthier and mightier Koord made a midnight raid upon their home, and carried off the beautiful mother.

GRACE ILLUSTRATED. 151

Whether Bayzie was more or less happy in her new home, or made any effort to return to her husband, we learn not; but he soon fled to Chemishgezek, where, at his death not long after, he left his two little orphans, servants in a wealthy Armenian family.[1]

The gospel light, and with it the idea of educating and elevating woman, which entered this home of "the Seven Young Confessors," so far penetrated this family, that Amy, the elder of the two girls, learned to read, and obtained a two-cent copy of the Gospel of Matthew. Our first knowledge of her was when (in 1869) a request came from Chemishgezek, that we receive "a poor girl" to the Harpoot Female Seminary.

Our reply was in the usual form: "If she

---

[1] By a misapprehension, it was stated in the Harpoot News, that "the father died, and the mother remarried;" which is true in reversed order of time.

is a suitable person, and any one is responsible for her clothes, books, and traveling expenses, we will receive her," adding, "but our seminary is not an alms-house." The reply soon came, "She is a poor Koordish girl, for whom no one cares; and those with whom she lives are so far from wishing to send her, that, should she go to school, they would even deprive her of all her best clothes."

Our reply, "Such a girl will not do for us to educate," put an end to the matter, till, some months later, Mr. H. N. Barnum and myself visited Chemishgezek; and Amy appeared before us to plead her own cause.

She seemed thoroughly possessed with the idea, that come she must to the seminary, — that paradise of girls in need of Christian education.

No Armenian girl of her age, unless educated in a Protestant school, would have ventured to say a word to us, or even to reply to a question; but this poor Koordish girl, with her inborn nature energized by earnestness of desire, stood and pleaded her cause with a boldness and perseverance which interested and surprised us.

But to all her pleadings we had a ready reply, till she exclaimed, "Missionaries, if Jesus were now on earth, and a poor girl like me wished to come to him, and learn about his salvation, don't you think he would receive her?" To this question, enforced by her earnest tones, and pleading face, we could not find it in our hearts to give the cold, logical reply, "Oh! you can learn about Jesus here, without coming to the seminary;" for she at least felt, that, surrounded as she was by merely nominal Christians, she could not learn his will. But, earnest and sincere as she appeared, we still had a lingering fear of being deceived in this our first experience with a Koordish candidate : so we inquired of all the "Protestant brethren," whether, so far as they knew, she was truthful, industrious, and faithful, and, in their opinion, sincere in her request, or whether she might wish to go to the seminary from mere curiosity, or in hope of living an easier life. When all gave decided testimony in her favor, we said, "We will run the risk, and make this one experiment. Let her come." Take her ourselves we could not.

But, surrounded as she was by those hostile to us and the evangelical faith, mere *letting* would not bring her. And the difficulty increased greatly, when word went forth among the many Koords in the city, "The 'hat-wearers' are about to carry off one of the tribe, and make her a Christian." So the poor orphan suddenly had plenty of friends, who, with loaded guns, let it be known that any one would take her away at the peril of his life; and, as Koordish guns have laid many a poor Armenian low in those wild regions, it was not surprising that sudden fear and trembling took possession of the Protestants who had secured her interviews with the missionaries. But it was surprising to see how suddenly the introduction of this new alkaline element of fear turned all their beautiful coloring to a somber blue. Accustomed as we are to the timidity and fickleness of this land, we were amazed to see, that, all at once, Amy, the paragon of excellence, had become a "lazy shirk, seeking to escape life's burdens by hiding herself in a seminary, under pretense of learning about Jesus."

When all these improvised arguments had been rebutted by recalling words just before uttered by the same men, one of them, a very zealous Protestant, but rather poor

Christian, heedlessly let the truth out, inquiring in a distressful tone, " Is that Koordish girl of so much importance, that, for her sake, you are willing to send our souls into eternity unprepared? Shall we be lost, that she may be saved?"—" Not at all," we replied; " but, having once conscientiously taken a position, no fear of Koordish guns can turn us from it. And perhaps the Master is taking this way to prepare you, sir, for heaven. So long as you feel that the hour of death is uncertain, there is little hope of your being any thing more than a Protestant. Perhaps a look down the muzzle of a gun is just the thing needed to wake you up to prepare to meet God. So, then, we still say, ' Let her come.' "

It remained, then, to decide how the thing should be done. To take her along ourselves would raise a mob, and perhaps hinder her leaving, besides lifting our *pro-*

tégée up with pride and self-conceit at the thought of being of so much consequence. During the sabbath services, we had been struck by the earnest looks of a man some fifty years old, to whom the Word seemed to be like cold water to a thirsty soul.

During all the discussion about Amy, he had sat a quiet, interested listener; but now, when the time for words had passed, and that for deeds had come, he rose and came forward, saying, " Missionaries, do you intend to let this girl come to the seminary?" On our replying in the affirmative, he, with a resolute, martyr look, added, " Brethren, I can not conscientiously allow her to be prevented from going. Tell all the Koords that I did it. I will take her to Harpoot. Let them kill me, if any one."

But we much preferred that nobody die, and that one member of the little community *should* run away. He was a man equally famous for enduring persecution, and notorious for lazy loafing, — one who made it a matter of principle to sponge his living out of Protestant preachers, and in various ways bring reproach on the Protestant name.

Now, thought we, is the time to feed two birds with one grain of wheat, by getting Amy to Harpoot, and Garabed so out of this city, that he will never dare to come back. So we whispered in his ear, "You bring her," and left.

But he was as shrewd as lazy, and at once posted off to the chief of Amy's tribe, the famous Ali Gako of Mr. Dunmore's day,[1] and obtained a paper authorizing him to take her to Harpoot to be educated by the missionaries.

With this to insure his own safety, he

[1] See Missionary Herald for 1855, pp. 55, 340; for 1857, pp. 219, 346; and, for 1858, p. 113.

mounted her on a mule, and fled from the city by night, and appeared the next day with his prize at the seminary door, which she entered with curiosity, expectation, and delight, little, if any, less than that with which she and we shall at last cross the threshold of the New Jerusalem. With her tall, erect form, dark, flashing eyes, long, rather coarse, unkempt hair, and (to a gentleman) indescribable toilet, coarse, ragged, and peculiar, our mountain maid was a subject for a painter. It hardly need be said, that entering the seminary with feelings such as hers, and brought daily, continually under the religious influences of the place, she, ere long, yielded her heart to the Saviour about whom she had come to learn. Some three years afterwards she was baptized, and entered into covenant with the church in Harpoot, of which she is still a member.

Her progress in study during the four years she was a pupil in the seminary was laborious, very slow, and very sure. Any thing once learned was learned for permanence and use. Once having acquired it herself, she was ready and able to teach others also; and when examining the girls' school, which, during the year past, she taught in Central Harpoot, we were both amused and gratified at seeing what a female seminary in miniature she had.

Each movement and method were after the exact model. And, before a crowd which would have abashed almost any other pupil, she, with the self-possessed dignity of an old, experienced teacher, went through the exercises.

One quality, rare enough in this land, but which she exhibited in Occidental measure, is that of steadfast performance of duty to be done, in spite of the efforts of others to turn her aside. It is a very, very difficult thing here to induce teachers to adhere to rules laid down for their government, and especially in regard to time. But when a person of some consequence once tried to induce Amy to omit a lesson at its time, and was angry with her for failing to comply with his wishes, she replied, " The missionaries have put me here to teach these girls; *and I shall do it.*"

Amusing as it may seem, she still entertains high ideas of her former condition, and speaks in lofty terms of " the big house " in which she had the honor of serving. A more prolific source of pride is in the attentions paid by many to " the Koordish girl," who is sure to be the first one sought out by visitors to the seminary, in which, during the present year, she has been made assistant teacher.

She has any but true ideas in regard to our

connection with her coming here. As she recently stated in a letter, "When the Harpoot missionaries learned of my desire to come to the seminary, two of them came to Chemishgezek to see me." (!) And were we to give her all the flattering messages sent by those in this land and at home, who feel an interest in her, and especially were she to hear all the noise that is made about her, she and we could with difficulty dwell in the same house.

The earnest spirit of emulation which has thus far characterized her leads her to aspire even to "complete her education" in some American South Hadley or Vassar.

Disappointed in her plans and efforts, or especially wounded in her sensitive-plant feelings, she sinks at times into what we call "the depths of indigo," tinged, now and then, with a hue of sanctimony, constraining the writer once to call to her, "Why, Amy, I thought you were about to die; and here you are again wickedly taking the air with these worldly-minded girls!"

But, though not yet blooming in the perfect beauty and symmetry of a flower of paradise, she is one who adds much to the attractions of our "missionary garden." Her evidently conscientious desire to do right, her patient, prayerful efforts to please her teachers as pupil, and now, as assistant teacher, to exert a Christian influence over those whom she instructs, and her humbling sense of her felt deficiencies, give ground to hope much for her future usefulness. Would that, with a suitable companion, she might return to labor for her own people, among whom the light of the gospel has hardly begun to shine!

Her one ungratified desire is to have her sister Hedjie a pupil in the seminary. Over this she anxiously meditates, and for it she prays. And if earnest, eloquent, gifted prayer avail, her request will surely ere long be granted ; for she knows how to plead with God as few or none of her sex here do. 'Tis said that already Hedjie has learned to read, and is watching her opportunity to escape from her semi-servitude, and join her sister here. But of this we know not. Those, certainly, with whom she is living, will take good care that she do not too easily fall into missionary hands.

Not so happy the fate of Rose, — we forget the Koordish of it, — a girl from a tribe residing some seventy-five miles north-east from Harpoot. Permitted by her parents to reside for a time in a Protestant family in the capital of the Geghi district, she formed the purpose, which we did not encourage, to come to the famous seminary. We advised, rather, that, for a time, she study in the school taught there by the pastor's wife.

But, poor girl! she was not allowed to do it; for her parents dragged her back to their mountain-home, where, against her wish, she was married to an untamed Koord.

Should any one ask why we did not at once take this poor girl to Harpoot, we reply, "Because we wished first to try her farther; and, secondly, because her tribe, being of the wildest sort, would certainly have avenged her coming by the blood of some one or more members of the family with whom she lived. Will not all who read this sketch join us in praying for the speedy dawning, on these mountain-fastnesses, of the day of religious liberty?

XIII.

A PILLAR REMOVED.

WHO shall tell us whether it is from the innate force of gospel truth to develop leadership, or by special providential appointment, that almost without fail, wherever a little body of believers is collected, an Aaron, with, perhaps, an added Hur, comes to the front as leader in church-work, whether of praying or practical working? Were all these earnest workers to be gathered in some one body, even a pretty large one, the effect might not be the best even there; while many a little leaderless band would lose heart and all aggressive force, and the little light in many a dark place go out.

Such a leader early appeared for the little Protestant band in the village of Hulakegh, about six miles west from Harpoot.

At one of Mr. Dunmore's earliest visits there, he was sought out by a man, Avak by name, who timidly purchased a Bible, and hurried away to hide it at a neighbor's house, where he might secretly go and read the forbidden book; for, though about forty years old, he was, according to Oriental custom, still subject to his father, who would not allow the "Prote Bible" to enter his house.

Being a church "reader," Avak had not to go through the usual tedious process of learning to read, but was able, from the first, to peruse his new-found treasure understandingly. Being a sincere, conscientious man, the result was, that he was soon known as an adherent of the new faith, of which, in spite of a somewhat phlegmatic, conservative turn of mind, he at once became an earnest, practical apostle, going from man to man, house to house, and village to village, as an unpaid preacher. And the character of these efforts was in marked contrast to those of some of his fellow Protestants, who were such merely. Inquired one of these one day, "How happens it that I have so much trouble, while you, who talk so much, get along so easily?" — "Oh!" replied Avak, "because you seek noise; and I, peace and success." — "I see," retorted the other, touched by the home-thrust, "you raise the plow at every stone, while I let it remain." — "Rather," replied Avak, "say that you use the ax on the stone." A result of his wise, loving efforts to win men, enforced by his consistent Christian example, was, that one, and another, and another were won to the new, old faith, who are now living members of the little Hulakegh church. The death of the father soon opened the way for bringing home the proscribed book, and made Avak, as oldest of three brothers, the head of a family of fifteen, who were soon united in studying and obeying the new book. Burning with zeal to fit himself for more effective preaching, he now entered the newly-opened theological seminary in Harpoot. But a month's trial convinced both him and us that he was out of his place; and he went back to labor on in the old way. The question of forming a church in Hulakegh was hard to decide, perhaps I should rather say *easy;* for, though the people were not poorer than the mass of those of other villages of Harpoot plain, they did seem to be more penurious, and to justify very little hope of their ever supporting a pastor. The decision turned, at last, upon the question, whether Avak and his brothers could be induced to pay the unprecedented sum, for a village family, of ten dollars a year. To our surprise and gratification, the presentation of the question to him in that form secured an immediate affirmative. He could do any thing necessary for such an object, and the church was formed; the village of which we had said, "No self-supporting church can ever be formed there," being among the first to assert its independence of foreign aid.

But the days of John Concordance and tithe-paying were first to come, and multiply this ten dollars by three and more.

One of John's converts, a student in the theological seminary, went to tell the people of Hulakegh of the new, easy, and equitable method of providing for church expenses. But for Avak to tithe the income of himself and brothers, and thus increase the ten to thirty-four dollars for the current year, was harder than to make the original contribution. So, in the meeting held to consider the question of tithe-paying, his natural conservatism came prominently out, and he was forward and efficient in offering objections to the new plan. "It would be difficult to tell the amount of the tithes," an objection, which, from a farmer, who would pay in kind, evidently originated more in the heart than the head. Then, "there would be danger of withholding the tithes, and, like the Jews, 'robbing God,' and falling under his wrath and curse," &c.

This dialogue between pulpit and pews — or, rather, seat on the floor, — went on till the young theologue summoned courage to say, "Brother Avak, it seems to me that only those who fear that God will give them a good deal are unwilling to return his tithes."

The arrow had reached the mark. His

better nature at once re-assumed the ascendency; and he exclaimed, " You are right!" and immediately rose, and began to pray, telling the Lord all about his past covetousness, and promising to do better in the future. And the vow then made he faithfully kept till his dying-day, which came in September, 1869, when he was suddenly prostrated with a disease which deprived him of the power of speech, which was restored to him only for a very brief period before his death. These moments he improved in expressing gratitude to God for giving him the power of speech once more, and telling those about him how much he should love once more to make a preaching-tour among the villages.

This testimony given, he closed his eyes and lips, to open them, we doubt not, amid the glories and praises of the better world, and leaving behind him a name which will long have a saintly fragrance in all the region around.

XIV.

DEACON AVEDIS.

THE little Hulakegh church had yet one more pillar; but of him, too, the Lord had need, and, in the September following the death of Avak, called him to higher service.

His was a later and somewhat peculiar conversion to the gospel faith. The work in the village began, and for some time continued, among *men* exclusively; and it was a happy day, when, by the use of a little worldly wisdom — taking a company of missionary ladies and Protestant "sisters" from Harpoot to a dedication service in the village, and so, by an appeal to innate curiosity, luring some *women* to that dreaded place, a

Protestant meeting — we succeeded in convincing a very few that those who read the Scriptures in the modern spoken tongue were not worse than Turks. Of those whom curiosity lured in, two or three, soon followed by a crowd, came again and again; and, ere long, Hulakegh was noted for the extent of the evangelical work among the women. Among those who first learned to read the gospel was the wife of Avedis, thereby so putting him to shame, that, he too, purchased a primer, and imitated her example.

The entrance of God's word gave not only intellectual light, but spiritual understanding; and he was soon so marked for his consistent, earnest Christian character, that, on the formation of the church in Hulakegh, he was chosen as its first deacon. But his was to be a very brief earthly service. While he lived, he gave himself, with all his heart, to the duties of his office, and to general evangelistic effort among all classes; so that, at his death, "all the village wept," Protestants and Armenians alike. His one thought was, "What more can be done to advance Christ's work among us?" But, in the autumn of 1870, he was seized with typhoid-fever, and felt from the first that his end was near. He had no fear of death, but calmly attended to all necessary business, as if he were but going on a journey. His greatest care was for the church; and, when reason was dethroned, the current of thought was still the same.

Now he was on the point of leaving his "dark, smoky, narrow dwelling, to go and dwell in a royal palace, full of light and glory," and was urging those about him to be ready to accompany him. Again he had "drunk to the fill of the living water which Jesus promised to the woman of Samaria," and invited others to drink too, and see how sweet it was; and yet again his couch was covered with every variety of beautiful and sweet-scented flowers from paradise; and he expressed surprise that those about him could not see and smell their beauty and sweetness as he did. Apparently almost entirely unconscious of pain, and reveling amid such delights, he was enjoying on earth rapturous foretastes of heaven. To all the church-members who visited him, his one charge was, "Care well for the church, and labor in hope. These clouds will soon all pass away, and God will again bless his own cause." When his wife inquired, "Why do you not talk to us?" he replied, "I do not need to do so. I have already, when in health, said enough to you; and now I only add, 'Let my death put the seal of truth to all my counsels.'"

Once only did he allude to his sufferings, saying, "My body is filled with pain, but

GRACE ILLUSTRATED. 177

my soul with joy." Unlike Avak, he declined to call a physician, saying it would do no good; and, when near his end, he set apart the sum he should have paid for medical service, saying, "Pay this for the missionary work in Koordistan."

At last, conscious that his end was near, he uttered a few last words to those about him, and adding, "I shall talk no more," closed his eyes in death. The most blessed memory which he left behind him was that of his character as the peacemaker. And he passed away at a time when a threatened division in the church seemed to plead most effectively for the longer tarrying of such as he. This second pillar removed, it almost seemed that the little church could not survive. But, though *the two leaders* were gone, there remained too many of kindred spirit, too many loving, praying Christian souls, men and women, and they are led by a pastor of too much Christian experience, to allow the candlestick to be removed out of its place.

XV.

DER KEVORK.

IN our ramble in the missionary garden, we shall light upon some specimens of doubtful genus, requiring the Master's analysis to decide whether they are plants of his, or only weeds. Such an one we have in Der Kevork ("Priest George").

On reaching Harpoot in 1857, we found in mission employ, and for the time being occupying the Harpoot pulpit, a man of about forty-five years, of a rather stout build, and sluggish movement, whose face wore a somewhat sinister look, together with one of triumph and self-satisfaction, which combined seemed to say, "I've won a victory, and got a reward, and am ready to tell all how to do the same." When sabbath came, and he rose to preach, his delight seemed to be to pound the pulpit with his clinched fist, and throw forth in a spiteful, son-of-thunder tone, sentences, which, I subsequently learned, were aimed against the absent sinners from whom he had so recently separated, the adherents of the Armenian Church, and particularly the priests and *vartabeds*, for whom no terms of condemnation seemed to him quite adequate. "This man," said I, "is a very pugnacious preacher. Pity he can't put a little more love into his tones." He soon came to call on the new missionary, and, sitting down by his side, began to rattle off a string of unintelligible sentences, taking it for granted, as do all in this land, that, of course, all Americans speak Armenian. Of one sentiment he resolved to compel an understanding by a slow, measured utterance of "Eench — vore

—emus—ay—koogut—ay,—yev—eench—vore—koogut—ay—emus—ay." Finding that decrease of his speed did not increase the force of my understanding, he opened the Testament at Acts iv. 32, and helped me to translate his utterance as "That which mine is yours is, and that which yours is mine is." There I had it. The preacher, like most of his class, a son of poverty and covetousness combined, not satisfied with the rather fat salary paid him from the missionary treasury, proposed to divide possessions with the new-comer from the golden-hilled land beyond the waters. This impression was confirmed, when, some days afterwards, he came to put his text into practical use by helping himself from the missionary wood-pile.

Observation during the week impressed me rather too forcibly with the idea that the new convert was lazy. "Too forcibly,"

I say; for to one fresh from live, stirring Yankee-land, all the Orient seems to be peopled with a dead-and-alive race; and, of course, any individual sluggard is comparatively *too* harshly judged. But years of observation have not only justified the opinion then formed, that this particular priest was covetous and lazy, but also that he is but a representative of his class. It would seem, that, by some mysterious process, the holy oil of consecration inoculates them all with these two incurable distempers. Suffice it to say that Der Kevork's frailties seemed day by day less hopeful of removal, and all the more so, because he imagined that the missionaries dare not offend a person of his importance. The wood-pile embargo weakened somewhat this confidence, which received a more violent shock when the missionaries took possession of the city pulpit, and he was located in the neighing village of Husenik, with instructions to open a school.

He must now make a demonstration suited to alarm his misguided employers, and bring them to terms,—more money, and less work, and that in the place of his choice, or let them tremble at the prospect of losing so important a proselyte.

So one day a good Protestant brother, with a face the image of despair and alarm, rushed panting into our house, and exclaimed, "Der — Kevork — is — parleying — with — the — Armenians!" The response of a hearty laugh and "Praise the Lord for it," was to him inexplicable trifling with a solemn matter; for he had no doubt that the breaking of such a pillar would bring a Dagon-temple ruin on the Protestant cause. But not so we. So when, shortly after, we received from him a letter, inquiring, "If I remain in your service hereafter, how much will my salary be?" we at once replied, "See Matt. xxvi. 15. Your salary will hereafter be five paras" (half a cent) "per month."

The result was his immediate employment by the Armenians of Husenik as their preacher, followed by a shout of triumph, to tell all the people that the Protestant cause was ruined.

So far there is nothing to show that our plant is any thing more than a mere weed, a tare of the enemy's sowing in the garden of the Lord. But here begins a different manifestation. While in missionary employ, his scanty store of preaching-material, and perhaps scantier supply of Christian charity, had constrained him to resort to that most abundant and accessible of all stores, — abuse of those who differ from us.

But, once more inside their church, he began to surprise all the Armenians, and offend many, by preaching to them the fervid and searching evangelical sermons which he had heard from the apostolic Dunmore. And the result was such a ferment in that town as years of missionary preaching could not have produced. Contrary to our expectation, he did not abuse the missionaries, nor say that we were in error. He only compromised with his own conscience by conforming to certain rites, and repeating certain petitions to the saints, which their church-service requires. The Armenians of Husenik had just built them a large and fine stone church; and their new preacher made its arches resound with truths new to the crowds who flocked to hear him.

The result was loud and bitter complaint by some, who exclaimed, "This Prote is leading us all astray from the faith of our fathers!" And when, one day, from some imperfection in its construction, the noble pile fell flat, just after the priest had been preaching, they declared that the bawling of that son of thunder had thrown it down.

He must preach smoother things, or lose his place. And preach them he did for a little time, till one day he rose in his place, and told a dream. During the preceding night he had died, and gone to the judgment-seat. With fear and dread, he heard the Saviour call one and another and another, and declare their eternal destiny for weal or woe, and bid the angels execute his sentence. Near the throne were seven yawning mouths of as many different hells; the seventh and deepest being reserved for unfaithful ministers of the gospel.

At length his own turn came, and, fixing, upon him a look of anger, the judge inquired, "Why have you ceased to preach to the people the truths which I bade you tell them?" "I was speechless," said he; "for

I had done this only to please you, and not to satisfy my conscience, and please my Master. So he called two mighty angels, and said to them, 'Take this unfaithful priest, and cast him into the seventh hell.'

"They seized me, and were dragging me towards the mouth, when, uttering a shriek of despair, I awoke. And now I can keep silence no longer. I must and shall tell you all the truth."

The result was, that the place soon became too hot for him; and he accepted a call to an Armenian church in Harpoot, where he remained ten years or more, preaching with more or less faithfulness, but with a conscience ill at ease from conformity to the customs of the church. On the approach of Easter, when all are expected to confess, and partake of the communion, his daughter once found him weeping over his Bible, and asked, "Father, why do you do these things, if they are against your conscience?"

"I would not," he replied, "if I were young, or had a grown-up son to care for me." While here, though his preaching had some awakening power upon the masses, who heard him gladly, and did many things, few, if any, did the one thing needful; for his practice in conforming to church mummery seemed to deprive the gospel word of its ultimate divine force to convert the soul. The result was the development of a pharisaical spirit of reform in some directions, while leaving the root of evil untouched.

Some, indeed, stirred by his preaching to hunger for the bread of life, found their way to the Protestant church; but, for the consciences of most awakened ones, he had some ready salve which was effectual in soothing them to rest.

If he ever himself felt the Spirit's power in his heart, his sinful compliance has so dulled his perceptions, and the teachings of his church (practically ignoring, if not denying, the work of the Spirit in days subsequent to the apostles) have so obscured his mental vision, that, instead of directing the troubled sinner to the only Physician, he finds for him in outward works an opiate for an awakened conscience.

But in Harpoot, too, difficulties arose; and, some months since, he accepted a call to Gaban Maden, where, doubtless, he will run much the same course, and go, ere many years, to that judgment-seat before which, in vision, he trembled and shrieked.

Fortunately we are not called upon to do Christ's work of judgment; for, "if we were," as a good old man once said, "we should let many into heaven who don't belong there, and keep out many who do."

XVI.

"THE LORD'S BEDROS."

Mr. DUNMORE had not been long in Harpoot, before he was able to write, that a "notorious tippler" had been won to the truth.

Nor were these early hopes to be disappointed. The tippler not only became and continued a sober man, but, infinitely better, a sincere Christian.

He at once began to devote a large part of his time to efforts to lead others to the truth, supporting himself and family by laboring a part of the time at his trade as a gunsmith. A man of much native tact and shrewdness, though uneducated, he soon became a walking concordance of the Scriptures; being always ready to give chapter and verse. He was, besides, entirely fearless in prosecuting his evangelistic labors; so that, ere long, Mr. Dunmore wisely judged that he should be employed as a permanent missionary helper; and from that day to this, eighteen years, he has, with the exception of one year, been thus employed, winning many souls to Christ, for, from the first, he fixed his heart on this single aim. His tact in so quoting Scripture as to silence opposers enables him to win his way where most would retire abashed; while his simplicity and earnestness of Christian character give him great power in convincing those who approach him. An incident in his early labors will illustrate this. He started for the village of Haboosie, distant some twelve miles from Harpoot, and meeting successively three men on the way, who inquired whither he was going, he was, on informing them, met by the reply

"There is a certain Torose there, by winning whom to Protestantism, you will convince us, also, of its truth. Bedros needed no other challenge to find out and labor for this wicked and apparently incorrigible opposer; and he was soon won, not only to Protestantism, but, better still, apparently to Christ; and, though his has been a hard fight against his old nature, such is his reputation for saintliness, that he has been called even by a sick priest to read and pray with, in hope of healing him.

If there be a stronghold of opposition, Bedros is the man to enter it, either by direct attack or by stratagem.

Such, for centuries, has been the haughty insolence of the Turks to the Armenians here, that, till the coming of missionaries, they did not even allow them to beat a *goachnag*, a piece of board used in some places to summon the people to church. In Harpoot city,

Mr. Dunmore first used such a board for his own meetings; and, in time, the Armenians followed suit.

It was a more difficult thing to introduce the custom in outlying places, and especially in Palu, where Bedros was for a time laboring, because the foolish Armenians, jealous of the Protestants for enjoying a privilege which they dared not claim, complained to the Turks that that Protestant was breaking the law; and the governor of the city forbade Bedros to beat his *goachnag* again. But, hearing that the pasha of the district was coming with a retinue of soldiers, he resolved by one bold stroke to stop the mouths of all opposers; and just as his Excellency, with all his retinue, came down the hillside opposite the Protestant church, Bedros went upon the roof, and gave out a loud, emphatic rub-a-dub-dub, rub-a-dub-dub, from his board, and then hastily descending, and outrunning the

Armenians who started to complain to the pasha, he paid his respects to him, and at once entered a complaint against them as men trying to restrain him in the enjoyment of his religious right to call his people together for worship. A stern rebuke to them, with an order to let him alone, sent them away unheard; and henceforth they, too, began to use a *goachnag*.

Calling once at a monastery, and upon a *vartabed*, a relative of his, he was rudely repulsed with, "You have apostatized: I don't know you."—"Very well," replied Bedros, "if I have strayed, you should have sought me. But, instead of this, I have sought you; and you must now by this gospel convince me of my errors." Ill prepared for a conflict with such a weapon, the *vartabed* fled to another room of the monastery, in which the Turkish governor of Palu was a guest. But Bedros was not to be shaken off so easily, and at once followed him. Being asked by the governor who he was, he replied, "I am a Protestant preacher of the gospel; but this Christian *vartabed* refuses me lodgings." — "Be my guest, then," he replied; and, turning to the *vartabed*, asked, "Is not your gospel the same?" He failing to answer, Bedros replied, "It is; but he does not receive it. To prove this, let him say whether some things which I say are not true." At this the governor laughed heartily, and said, "Say on." — "First of all, then," said Bedros, "the gospel says, 'If thine *enemy* hunger, feed him; if he thirst, give him drink:' but this *vartabed* does not receive us, though we are his *friends* and relatives." At this the governor said to the *vartabed*, "You have done wrong, and should repent," at which the latter left in confusion, but soon returned, and beckoned Bedros to follow him, who, having taken supper with the governor, did so. Seated in another room, the *vartabed* told Bedros that he did not hate, but pity, him for his errors. "Convince me of them, then, by this book," was the instant reply of Bedros, pulling out his Testament. "I will try," replied the *vartabed*. "Tell me, then, whence you have authority to preach the gospel?"—"Here in 1 Pet. ii. 9," was the ready reply, "it is said to *common Christians*, 'Ye are a chosen generation, a *royal priesthood*, . . . that ye should show forth the praises of him who hath called you out of darkness into his marvelous light.' In Acts viii. 4, we read that *common Christians* went everywhere preaching the word. And here in 1 Pet. iv. 10, 'tis said, 'As *every man* hath received the gift, even so minister the same one to another.'" Unable to meet this array of texts, the *vartabed* changed the subject. Another *vartabed* coming in, and the servants of the monastery gathering around them,

Bedros then spent four hours in faithfully preaching the gospel, and at the close was followed to his room by a white-haired old man, who, telling him of a pilgrimage made by him to Jerusalem in the vain hope of finding peace of conscience, added, "I am ignorant. I do not know the way of salvation. Will you tell me what I must do to be saved?"

The poor old man listened as for his life, while Bedros told the story of the cross, and, at the close, exclaimed, "Alas! I have lost my days!" and continued asking questions till past midnight.

Warned by the people of Palu to desist from a proposed journey into the mountainous district to the north, as two men had just been robbed and murdered there, he assured them that he was ready not only to be robbed, but to die if need be, for the sake of preaching the gospel to his perishing countrymen in that district. So go he did, and fell into the hands of the Koords, six of whom, entering a house where he was a guest, robbed him of his watch and *aba*, a sort of cloak.

To the expostulations of the host, the robber chief replied, " Were God to come down from heaven, he could not prevent our taking what this man has."

He then demanded the rest of Bedros' clothes, and his money, which he refused to give up, unless force were used; and then he so set the robber's sin before him, and so excited his fears by appealing to the Mohammedan belief, that, at the judgment, the wicked must make good all the wrong inflicted on others, that he recovered back his watch and *aba*. His argument, in short, was this, " Do you believe there is a God ? " — " Yes." — " Will all men die ? " — " Yes." — " And be judged ? " — " Yes." — " They will indeed," continued Bedros; "and what then can you do? If a naked man were in the water, and ten men, pointing their swords at his breast, should say, ' Give us one para,' " (a tenth of a cent), " ' or we will kill you,' could he give it?"—"No," replied the Koord. "So you," continued Bedros, " will be naked before God in the judgment, when he shall demand of you this watch and *aba*, and, on your failing to restore them, send you to the place of everlasting torment."

The result was, that the Koord, having returned what he had taken, begged a copy of the Testament, from which Bedros went on to preach to him till half-past three o'clock in the morning, when the robber lay down to rest. But Bedros, though a firm believer in the perseverance of the saints, fearing that this unclean spirit had only left for a time, sat and watched his sleeping convert till dawn, who, on waking, began with much delight to show his Testament to his companions, and to tell them of the wonderful truths which Bedros had told him from it. At leaving, Bedros still feared that the robbers would intercept and rob him on his journey, as they had once before done to a guest, when bribed by the host to let him depart in peace; but his fears were groundless. And thus summer and winter, during most of these long years, sometimes through the pathless snows of the mountains, and often in perils of robbers, but never robbed, he has come and gone with a burning apostolic zeal which deservedly won for him the name, "Apostle." A little missionary girl five years old was so impressed by what she heard of his Christian zeal, that hearing us address him as Bedros, and curious to know whether he was *the* one, inquired, "Are you the Lord's Bedros?" He "hoped he was," and so do we assuredly. Sure we are that he has been instrumental in leading many to Christ. In these latter days, with the weight of years increasing upon him, his vigor and efficiency, if not his zeal, have been less conspicuous; but he seems to be the Lord's Bedros still, aiming with singleness of purpose to do the work which the Master gives him.

XVII.

"THIEF MAGHAK."

AND a shrewd, sharp one he was, till the gospel got hold of him, which it began to do in one of his oil-peddling tours.

From that day he became so upright in his dealings as even to redeem from reproach the more contemptuous name of "Prote [1] Maghak," which his adherence to the gospel fixed upon him. Even discussions over rites and ceremonies, usually worse than useless, can be useful, as was seen in his case. Perhaps we should rather say, that passages from God's word are so gemlike in their luster as to glitter even when cast among such rub-

---

[1] An abreviation of "Protestant," but so pronounced as to mean "pōrōde," a "leper."

THIEF MAGHAK.

bish. Being present at such a discussion in the village of Ichmch, Maghak's attention was drawn to a passage quoted by one of the disputants: "Now the Spirit speaketh expressly, that, in the latter times, some shall depart from the faith, . . . forbidding to marry, and commanding to abstain from meats." He came away, saying to himself, "These false teachers can not be the so much reviled Protestants; for their missionaries are married, and they make no rules about abstaining from meats; while our bishops and *vartabeds* never marry, and are very scrupulous about meat-eating on certain days." The result of these meditations was, that he resolved to obtain a "Protestant Bible," and examine for himself; and, though knowing not a letter of the alphabet, he at once bought the book, adding its key, a primer. Putting the latter in his bosom while on his peddling tours, and exacting a lesson from every reader to whom he sold his sesame oil, he was soon able, though stammeringly, to study the Bible for himself. The change was immediate and complete. From being notorious for dishonesty, he became equally famous for integrity in his dealings; so that even the Turkish owner of the soil which he and his brothers cultivated ceased to measure his share of the crop, taking Maghak's word for it. Soon his two brothers, and all the members of their united households, became adherents of the despised faith, now no longer despised in this region; for such has been the power of the gospel in externally saving people from the power of wickedness, that, alike among Mohammedans and nominal Christians, Prote no longer means leper, but an adherent of a purer faith than that of the mass.

Maghak still lives, though too feeble for any service, except that of illustrating the power of divine grace by a consistent Christian life.

He can not long survive; but while the smoky light of his sesame oil is giving place to the still more smoky emanations [1] of kerosene, and the oil-trade fast becoming a thing of the past, many a year must go by ere the light of the oil-peddler's life shall cease to shine in his native village, and others which have been reached by his story.

[1] As the kerosene is burned in common wick lamps, and usually with the wick pulled high up, the already blackened rafters of Oriental village homes are rapidly enriching themselves with a more luxurious accumulation of the essential soot.

XVIII.

DIVERSE GIFTS.

THE village of Shukhaji, perched upon the sides of a spur of the Taurus Mountains, some twenty miles east of Harpoot, early enjoyed the advantage of missionary labor by the location there of a native helper by Mr. Dunmore, the first missionary in the Harpoot field. And while, for several reasons, and among these the death of two native laborers successively located there, the gospel fruit has not been as abundant as we desire, it has furnished rather striking specimens of Christian life, two of which, by their contrasted character, suggest the heading given above. The first man to declare himself an adherent of the gospel was a hardy muleteer, Arakial ("Apostle") by name, whose nature and vocation had combined to make a resolute, independent, hard-headed, stout-handed man, with whom few cared to come into conflict. And, when the gospel took hold of his sturdy manhood, it took strong hold, and kept it. Everybody knew that that muleteer was an adherent of the new doctrines.

A brother's wife, residing in the same house, soon followed him, and suffered what he could not, — persecution. This woman was an especial object of hatred to Arakial's wife, by whom, in the absence of the husband, she was treated in a shamefully cruel manner. Resolved to put an end to this, Arakial, on his return, gave his wife a whipping, which cured her of her propensity (or, at least, the indulgence of it) to torment her sister-in-law. When expostulated with by Mr. Dunmore for this energetic method of administering family discipline, he replied, "Oh! I was only giving her a needed curtain-lecture." The native helper dying, the villagers rose in force to prevent his burial; but going himself, and digging a grave, he stood by it, pickax in hand, requesting any one of the mob who desired to be buried first to come on at once. The young preacher was buried in peace.

And our new convert was equally zealous in effort to lead others to the truth, though, in doing so, he showed himself somewhat of a "son of thunder," presenting quite freely the aggressive, vindictive side of the gospel, and being a little too much inclined to blame people for not coming to the light as readily and quickly as had he.

He still lives, and, while enfeebled by age and hard fare, is the same unflinching adherent of truth and right as he understands it, and in his deep poverty makes sacrifices for the gospel's sake, some of which would not be appreciated in enlightened Christian lands; such, for instance, as giving a rich young preacher a *valuable* daughter *gratis*, instead of taking from thirty to fifty dollars, as those villagers not adhering to the gospel, and perhaps even some professing to do that, would have done.

Come we now to one whose nature and gifts are diverse from these. Hazar was no "son of thunder," but a man of peace, of a gentle, loving temper, ruled less by impulse than by conscience. A younger brother in a large, and, for that place, wealthy family, he, by his quiet sincerity and energy, took the place of leader, and had almost undisputed control of the family property. There was one thing, however, which he could not control, — a wife as little inclined to gospel ways as was she whom Arakial ruled; and the result is, that, while the latter soon changed her naughty ways, the former holds to hers still.

Hazar, having been a "reader" in the old church, was at once ready for reading and receiving the Scriptures in the modern tongue.

A visit to his home would have given one a vivid idea of the diminutive amount of real comfort which even wealth usually purchases in this land. Wrote a missionary lady who visited it, "We went to Hazar's house, or rather hovel. As we entered, six men were taking breakfast at one table; and seven women, in another place, had their food upon the floor; while four dirty urchins occupied another part of the room. It was a scene. Poor man! he does not get much comfort at home. But his trials have been sanctified to him; for I never saw a more exemplary Christian. Of course, my testimony alone would not be sufficient to warrant the declaration; but all others give him the same character."

The " trials " alluded to were from a long and expensive conflict in the effort to erect a parsonage and a church, in which he took the lead, and which made sore drafts on both patience and purse; he having personally contributed three hundred and fifty dollars, while all the property of the family would, probably, not exceed fifteen hundred dollars. And yet we, who were deeply interested in the case, and doing what we could to help it on, did not know till afterwards how much it had cost pecuniarily and otherwise, so equable and calm was his temper, and so unassuming his manner at all times. He had consecrated himself and his all to Christ, and took it for granted that the consecration was accepted.

If there was any thing which we would have changed, it was this perfect uniformity.

Had he sometimes made his family piety a little less patient, a little more forcible and aggressive, he might have seen greater changes for the better in his large family circle. Said a quiet, patient saint to a restless, aggressive "son of thunder," "You do a great many things to harm Christ's work." — "And you," was the not less truthful reply, "*neglect* a great many things to harm it."

This remark might have been made with some justice of Hazar; but, take him all in all, he was a very good man, — one of whom it was justly said, "I never saw a more exemplary Christian," and "All give him the same character."

His one great aim, prayer, and effort was, that Christ's work might advance.

But just when he seemed indispensable to this progress, just when the struggle over the church and parsonage was over, and we began to hope that an independent church would soon be formed in Shukhaji, he was laid upon a bed of sickness, and at once said, "I shall not rise from it, but shall die." Fearing lest members of the family might, after his death, cause trouble to the little Protestant community, by laying claim to the property for which he had paid so heavily, he took pains to make all legally safe.

Some years before, he had joined the Harpoot church, but subsequently transferred his membership to the church in Ichmeh, nearer his home. But, upon his sick-bed, he recalled his old love, and, on the fifteenth day of his illness, sent to the Harpoot church a special message of affection, adding, "Tell them, that, though I am to die to-night, I have never been so peaceful as now." And so he did die that night, peacefully trusting in Christ to the last. In vain the old priest came, and begged to aid in saving his soul, saying, "Open your mouth, that I may give you the communion,—a piece of the body of Christ." He patiently allowed him to read and go through the mummeries of his church, keeping his mouth closed alike for communion and rebuke. He knew in whom he had believed, and knew, also, that the old priest could do him neither good nor harm. To avoid an unseemly quarrel, the priest was also allowed to commit the body to the grave with the same harmless forms; for we knew that the soul was safe in the hands of Him who had bought and cleansed it with his own blood.

XIX.

GRACE ABOUNDING.

BY MRS. O. P. ALLEN.

SEVENTEEN years have passed since the first prayer-meeting was established at Harpoot. In its early history, one chilly day in December, when the spacious room was crowded with eager listeners, the attention of the missionary was arrested by one who was present for the first time. Her fine intellectual countenance, dress, and grace of manner, were in striking contrast to most of those around her. In conversation with her after the meeting, she showed no signs of interest in the truth which had been uttered; and there was little expectation that she would come again. But in this case, as it too frequently happens, we failed to recognize the power of Him who holds the hearts of all in his hand, and is able to turn them whithersoever he will. From that time till her death (in 1871), she was in constant attendance, with the exception of the first three years, when she was occasionally absent, and during which time the truth seemed to make no impression on her heart. She was devoted to the world. She listened attentively to religious conversation and the reading of the Scriptures, and became familiar with the great truths of salvation, but manifested a stern determination to resist entreaties to seek Christ.

But the Holy Spirit came, and she was led to see her sin and danger. She fled to the cross, and there found the joy of forgiven sin. The change in her life was very marked. From a proud, worldly woman, she became a humble and self-denying Christian.

The things she counted gain before were now loss. She remarked, one day, to a friend, that her husband was urging her to prepare a marriage-outfit for Hanum (her daughter); but, said she, "I tell him it is not well to lay up treasures upon earth, where moth and rust doth corrupt." And she could not be prevailed upon to make the quantity of clothes the custom required, and which she was amply able to do, for the sole reason that she did not think it worthy an immortal soul to spend so much time on that which was to perish so soon.

One of the first lessons that the Spirit taught her was, that not only she herself, but all she called her own, belonged to Christ.

To the poor she gave frequently and freely, and with her own hands, but made others almoners of her contributions for the cause of Christ. Many a gold coin she brought to the pastor's wife, saying, "You know better than I what part of the work of the Lord is most needy." It was sufficient for her to know that the money went into the treasury of the Lord. Her children, too, were consecrated to the Master. Her eldest son fitted for the work of the ministry; but, health failing, he was not able to preach, and yet was able to give instruction in both seminaries for several years. One daughter became the wife of a preacher. Both she and her husband, this year, have joined the mother in the better land.

Mariam was the wife of a watchmaker, Puroodian by name. She prayed with an intense longing for the conversion of her husband; but the "convenient time" did not come till years afterward. One day, during a religious awakening, she came to the prayer-meeting, and, with a voice choking with emotion, begged the sisters to pray for her husband. The request was heeded; many fervent prayers being offered in his behalf. The next day he asked his son to pray with him, saying that his family were all going to heaven, but that he was doomed to perdition. At the meeting the following week, she came with a joyful heart, to praise God for his mercy in bringing him to Christ.

For years she was in feeble health, being a victim to a lingering consumption. She was often prostrated by disease, but, if she had power to walk about, was sure to come to the place of worship. She loved the prayer-meeting; and neither storms nor cold kept her at home. A year before her death, one wintry day, she came into the meeting, so exhausted from the effort to ascend a steep hill, that she could not speak for some moments. One remarked to her, "You are not able to walk such a distance." She replied, "What shall I do? I have a great desire to come." During the following winter, she became very sick, and her friends gave up all hope of her recovery. But she again rallied; and once more hope revived.

One morning, shortly after, a request came to the pastor and wife to visit her. As they entered her room, she said to them, "I am a pilgrim. I am going. I wish you to forgive me, if in any way I have wronged you, or injured your feelings." She had always treated them with the greatest kindness. They never visited her without receiving some token of her love, not given on the impulse of the moment, but something reserved especially for them.

She was sitting up in bed, and seemed as well as usual; and her friends tried to assure her that she was so. But she confidently affirmed that it had been revealed to her that night, that she was soon to leave them. She wished that all her relatives and acquaintances be called; and from them she sought forgiveness for every unkind word. She distributed the gold coins of her necklace among her friends, giving to her pastor's family several pieces as memorials of her love. The poor received from her own hands her clothes, with the exception of one suit. When the last garment had been disposed of, she smilingly said, "I have nothing left, except the clothes for my burial."

For a season, darkness came over her. She — to use her own words — "lost her Jesus." But the clouds soon dispersed; and He in whom her soul had taken great delight stood forth more glorious than ever before. She sent for her pastor, and, with a countenance beaming with joy, said, as he sat beside her, "I have all things now. I have found my Jesus: I have found my

Jesus! He left me for a little while; but he has returned." From that time till her death, a few days after, her mind was in "perfect peace." Death had no terrors for her. It was only the door through which she would enter into the " many mansions." It was her great desire that her pastor should perform her burial service; but it so happened, that there was to be a meeting at a place some three days' distant from Harpoot. The day for starting had been fixed. Should the pastor go, and leave this dying saint? He presented the case before her, and asked what he should do. "Go," was her quick reply. "Of course, you must go. Shall the work of the Lord be hindered for me? It will make but little difference who buries my poor body." So the pastor bade her a last good-by.

The following morning she sweetly and peacefully fell asleep.

"Asleep in Jesus! oh, how sweet
To be for such a slumber meet!
With holy confidence to sing
That death has lost its venomed sting."

XX.

PATIENT SARKIS.

THE wind, bearing the thistledown away over hill and dale, deposits its seed to grow and multiply on the distant mountain-side; or, better still, the little bird places beside it the seed of some fruit-bearing tree, brought from far, for a slower growth and a richer fruitage to bless men of coming time: but more mysterious and blessed still is God's providential work of scattering the good seed of his word at times. Some seventy-five miles north-east from Harpoot, hemmed in among the Anti-Taurus Mountains, and surrounded on all sides by Koords, are some thousands of Armenians, scattered over a district of some four hundred square miles, mostly isolated from the mass of the nation, and, till within a few years, sunk in the deepest spiritual ignorance, and fanatically attached to their national church. About twenty-five years ago, Sarkis, an inhabitant of the *Kasabah,* or chief town of this district, visited Constantinople, and, while there, received a present of a Testament, which, though unable to read, he took home, and hid in his house; for no one there might then with safety declare himself the possessor of the hated Protestant book.

The mass of the people were in the same condition of ignorance: but a few persons, called *deratsoos,* specially trained for aiding the priests in reading the church service, were possessed of the wonderful power of reading. To one of these he at length intrusted the secret of the strange book, and begged him to read it to him.

Then the good seed of the Word, so providentially wafted hither from far away, began to take root, and spring up. Others joined the reader and listener; and soon there was a little company who held secret meetings for reading. But secret they could not long remain; for the words they heard were as fire shut up in their bones.

This was especially true of Sarkis, whose *heart* was touched, and with meekness and courage he began to tell all abroad the contents of the wonderful volume, which he himself soon learned to read. As this must be stopped, the priests and the chief man of the town headed a mob, who went to the house of Sarkis, beat him, cast him into prison, and, making a fire in a public place, threw his Testament into it.

The imprisoning and beating were repeated again and again, but all to no purpose. Like the apostles before the sanhedrim, he replied, " Whether it be right in the sight of

God to hearken unto you more than unto God, judge ye. For I can not but speak the things which I have heard." To supply the place of the burned Testament, he went three days' journey to Erzroom, and purchased another, to which he afterwards added a Bible, and was known by all as a Protestant.

Meanwhile, the son of the leader of the mob, a young man, Hampartsoom ("Ascension") by name, attached himself to the gospel party, and was told by his father that he must forsake the society of Sarkis, and leave off reading the forbidden book, or leave his house. But, when he took his wife's hand to depart, the father's heart relented. The father and an elder brother having died not long after, Hampartsoom, without professing to be a Protestant, began to hold meetings at his house for Scripture-reading. As the priests dare not touch a man of his wealth and influence, one step was gained in the direction of religious liberty, — the right to read the Bible.

But it would have been amusing, had it not been painful, to see the timidity of these Bible-readers. In 1858, accompanied by the present pastor of the Harpoot church, I started to visit the place; but when in Temran, some nine miles distant, we were met by Sarkis, who had come as their delegate, to request, that unless proposing to remain in the *Kasabah*, so as to protect them, we would not visit the place, and thus stir up against them the enmity of the people.

To this we, of course, replied, "We come not for you alone, but for all the people; and if you are afraid of being called our friends, and suffering persecution, you are at liberty to stay away." At first, all except Sarkis did stay away; but sixteen of them speedily repented of their cowardice, and, furnishing us with a room of their own, treated us as their guests. Among these was not Hampartsoom, though apparently not from fear of persecution, but, rather, fearing loss of influence for good, as he called it; but during our week's stay there, uniformly at nine, P.M., he rapped at our doors, and remained till the night was far spent, conversing on gospel truth. "These sixteen," said he, "are now able to stand; and I commit them to you, and go back to the church to win others." Poor man! In vain we tried to show him the sin and danger of his course. Before we left the place, he made us a great feast, to which were invited some of the chief dignities of the town, for Oriental courtesy required this of him. And, at our subsequent visits to the place, he was uniformly friendly, at times even attending the Protestant meetings; but, to the time of his death, he retained his connection with the Armenian Church, seeming to have no deep heart-experience of the power of evangelical truth; and, now that he is gone, his sons seem to be still further removed from its influence.

The contrast between him and Sarkis was from the first marked. With the latter, there was no attempt to serve two masters. While so patient as to bear for many years persecution of the most violent kind, without indulging any bitter feeling towards his persecutors, and so timid and self-distrusting, that, even to this day, 'tis said that he reads family prayers from a prayer-book, yet, in all efforts to promote the gospel cause, he is an earnest, efficient leader, his timidity and self-distrust all disappearing when action is called for.

Hard and long was the contest against enemies who were resolved to prevent it, before the little church-building was erected, and longer and more trying still the struggle before a person suited to be pastor of the prospective church was secured, and his salary made up. But at length the end was gained; and, some months since, a fruit of that one Testament appeared in the formation of a church of twenty-four members from the *Kasabah* and neighboring towns, with the prospect of, ere long, forming another in Temran, while the leaven has spread extensively throughout the district, two other towns in which are occupied by evangelical laborers.

Meanwhile a rich blessing has come upon the family of Sarkis. His wife, an earnest Christian, went once rejoicing down to death's door, but was raised up to see one of her two daughters graduate from Harpoot Female Seminary, and return to marry their young pastor, and the other now one of the most promising pupils in the seminary, both sincere Christians. But his richest blessing is in seeing the moral reformation which has followed from that Testament so providentially placed in his hands, and which, having drawn in its train hundreds of Bibles and Testaments, and thousands of other volumes, — primers, copies of "Saints' Rest," Doddridge's "Rise and Progress," "Pilgrim's Progress," hymn-books, catechisms &c., — has inaugurated a moral change in that hitherto benighted district, which is but faintly indicated by the fact of the formation of the little church. Years ago, when a sermon was preached there on the sin of lying, and applied by saying, "You know that all of you except Sarkis are liars," no one took offense; but to make such an application now would be both unjust and unsafe; for a moral sentiment has arisen in the community, and a public opinion, which, while it demands truthfulness, at least, from the professed friends of the gospel, makes them resent the imputation of falsehood.

And by the side of the patient man, after so many years of unwearied waiting and working, stand at length some others whose hearts are moved only less deeply than his own, to see the entire district renovated by the gospel. And we trust the number will go on increasing, till even the surrounding Koords shall feel the influence of that Testament in the hands of Sarkis, and of his patient waiting, praying, and toiling.

"There shall be an handful of corn in the earth upon the top of the mountains; the fruit thereof shall shake like Lebanon."

XXI.

THE DESPAIRING SILVERSMITH.

THE modern gospel-net, equally with that of apostolic days, gathers some fish fit only to be cast away. If, then, we are to give a fair sample of our saints, or, rather, if we are so to gather our bouquet as to show honestly what is growing here in the garden of the Lord, we must pluck this one evident *weed;* for among the weeds we must surely class this one, unless we suppose the heavenly analysis to differ essentially from ours.

In our earlier missionary days, most of the native helpers were men of little or no education; some of them knowing little more than to read the Scriptures. Among those thus employed and sent forth, was a native of Gaban Maden, who, upon the decline of that place, had removed to the vicinity of Harpoot, and connected himself with the church here. Being a man of considerable personal presence and fluent speech, and, withal, quite zealous for the new faith, he was employed, and sent to labor in Ichmeh, a town which had a visitation of at least two worthless, if not harmful, laborers before it was blessed by the coming of "Little Gregory," its present pastor. Garabed the silversmith went; but the work did not open; and, on visiting the place, we had not far to look for the cause.

The zealous brother was a lazy, inefficient laborer; and when he did, now and then, wake up, it was only to discuss questions of form and ceremony with the Armenians. In vain we urged him to let alone the fasts, "which even heathen Turks eat," and point the people to Jesus.

The poor man did not seem to know the way. Alas! he had himself been converted (?) under the labors of one whose first sermon to the people of Maden had been acted in a coffee-shop by cooking and eating an egg on a fast day. So we called him back to work at his trade as a silversmith, at which he was so much offended, as, to his dying-day, to look upon us with no kindly eye. It soon appeared that the gospel had not made him a more honest man than before, when he had weighted the silver with excessive alloy. When expostulated with, he made the usual apology of such sinners, — that he must live in some way, and could not do it honestly at that trade; for, were he to be honest, people would not believe it. But at length he had a call to what promised to be a more gainful pursuit.

The people of the neighboring town of Yegheki, so roused by rumors of the new gospel as to wish to hear it, and yet unwilling to break away from their own church, and bear the reproach of being Protestants, invited the silversmith to become their preacher on condition of his putting in the usual alloy of crosses, fasts, and other superstitions. He accepted their call, and labored among them a year, when he returned to his old trade and old ways. But ere long he was laid upon a sick-bed, from which he was not to rise. For a time, he seemed unconscious of his sickness alike of body and soul, but at length awoke to feel them both.

Summoning a Protestant Christian physician, he piteously begged him to heal him. The physician plainly told him the truth, saying, "If you have any preparation to make for death, now is the time to make it."

At length, mortification began in one of his hands; and as it slowly crept up along his arm, and neared his vitals, he pointed visitors to his decaying, loathsome body, saying, "God is making me a spectacle for all to behold and fear, that others may not do as I have done." His groans were doleful to hear. In vain did one and another Christian visitor point him to Christ as still willing to hear and save him, if he would but look to him. "Christ," he replied, "has turned his face away from me. My time of repentance is past. It is too late, too late!" And in this state he closed his eyes in death, and passed to the tribunal of Him against whom he had so grievously sinned.

"If we sin willfully after that we have received the knowledge of the truth, there remaineth no more sacrifice for sins, but a certain fearful looking-for of judgment and fiery indignation which shall devour the adversaries. He that despised Moses' law died without mercy under two or three witnesses: of how much sorer punishment, suppose ye, shall he be thought worthy, who hath trodden under foot the Son of God, and hath counted the blood of the covenant, wherewith he was sanctified, an unholy thing, and hath done despite unto the Spirit of grace?" Of such a one Watts well says, —

"What scenes of horror and of dread
Await the sinner's dying bed!
Death's terrors all appear in sight,
Presages of eternal night.

His sins in dreadful order rise,
And fill his soul with sad surprise;
Mount Sinai's thunders stun his ears,
And not one ray of hope appears.

Tormenting pangs distract his breast;
Where'er he turns he finds no rest.
Death strikes the blow — he groans and cries,
And in despair and horror — dies."

XXII.

THE KOORDISH MISSIONARY.

AMONG the Koordish-speaking students gathered by the churches of Harpoot, to be trained in the theological seminary here for prosecuting their prospective missionary work in Koordistan, was a young man, Kavmè Ablahadian, a native of Cutturbul on the Tigris.

Like most residents in that Babel town, he had the gift of tongues, readily speaking Turkish, Arabic, and Koordish, to which he soon added Armenian, and, subsequently, some knowledge of English. Though a zealous, warm-hearted adherent of evangelical truth, and burning with desire to prosecute the missionary work in the regions beyond his native borderland of Koordistan, he soon became convinced that he was not experimentally a Christian, and, with deep anxiety, asked, "What must I do to be saved?" Under the faithful instructions of the Harpoot pastor, himself a native of Hainè in Koordistan, and so acquainted with the Koordish, he soon came out into the clear light of gospel liberty. His was a deep, old-style experience of something more than mere sentiment. His intellect enlightened by the teachings of the Bible, his sensibilities deeply moved by gospel manifestations of divine love, and his will completely subjected to divine direction, and fixed in purpose of service, he consecrated his whole being to the service of Christ. No one will imagine from this that he became at once, or has yet become, a perfect character, any more than do others here, and elsewhere, by a similar experience.

Were it necessary to do so, I could point out marked deficiences, showing especially how feeble even a partially sanctified and confirmed Oriental will is, to stand firm in defense of a purpose which is assaulted by excited sensibilities; but our present purpose leads not that way.

During his course of study, he spent one winter vacation in Shemshem, a polyglot town in Koordistan, and succeeded in winning his way to some hearts which were hard to enter; and one in Sinamood, a ward of Harpoot, being prevented by his wife's illness from going to the more distant place. At his graduation, the people of Sinamood pressed their claim so forcibly, that, seeing the Koordish mission treasury poorly supplied with funds, he consented to remain with them a year, they assuming his entire support. But, being permitted to make a visit to his beloved Koordistan on condition that he should not remain there, he kept his pledge in the letter, but broke it in spirit, by making a like promise to the little Protestant community in Redwan, one of the Koordish missionary stations of the Armenian churches.

Among the mingled population of Armenians, Jacobites, Koords, Turks, and Yezidees in that dark center of Koordistan proper, the gospel had gained an entrance; and a congregation of eighteen men, thirteen women, and twenty-two children, had separated themselves from the superstitions of their people, erected a little church, and, deprived of their former preacher (who had gone to another station), begged Kayme, to stay, saying, "We will pay half of your salary now, and all by and by, and will build you a house. Do come! Do not leave us alone." The result was, that he hastened back, said "Good-by" to his city parish, and hurried off for Redwan,— as great a descent externally as for a New York pastor to leave his fine mansion, and go to dwell in one of the "sod houses" of Dakota, with the added fact, that the contrast between the people of Harpoot and those of Redwan is little, if any, less than that between their dwellings.

But not thus was he to remain at rest. A "call" followed him from the city of Diarbekir, which he at once laid before his people, who had meantime, self-moved, increased their half of his salary to four-sevenths. Their reply was, "The Diarbekir people need you very much; and we will lend you to them for a few months." He came; but some of the Diarbekir people, on seeing him, almost repented the call. He was very unassuming, at times seeming almost to beg pardon of men for the offense of being among them.

But a few weeks' experience changed all that feeling on the part of the people; and, at the expiration of the allotted time, only a sense of honor and necessity made the city parish willing to return the loan. Said a hitherto somewhat phlegmatic brother, "I have listened for years to the learned, eloquent sermons of our pastor, Mr. ———, and they only pleased, without benefiting me; but this man talks to me about myself, and the salvation which I need. *He is doing my soul good.*" And so he was. Ah! after all, the primary preparation for a useful gospel ministry is a deep heart-experience of the power of the doctrines of grace. This can vivify and clarify the sleepiest and muddiest brain, and energize the feeblest, almost supplying that which is wanting, and setting it at work for Christ; while without it the most resplendent talents can only please the ear, and inform the mind, leaving the heart unbenefited and unreached.

But we found Kavme, ill at ease in his city parish. He longed to return once more to his humble Koordish congregation. And the way was providentially opened for him soon to do so. He goes fully purposed to be an earnest, self-denying, Christian missionary there.

May God give him health and long life, and the needed wisdom and grace for carrying out his purpose! Will not all the readers of this brief sketch unite with us in this petition.

XXIII.

THE LITTLE SYRIAN MAID.

BY MISS M. E. WARFIELD.

(From the Christian Mirror.)

DEAR S. S. CHILDREN,—Would you like to enter an upper room, where I went, a short time since, to the death-bed of one of our loved pupils? She was lying, according to the custom of the people, upon the floor. The father, also upon the floor, was sitting at her head. The mother, assistant teacher, the pastor and wife, and a few other friends, were gathered around to watch the loved daughter, whose life was fast passing away.

Her eyes were covered, and she lay perfectly quiet; while the difficult breathing showed that she could not long remain. It was painful to witness the distortion of her bright face at every breath. We supposed she was entirely unconscious to all earthly things: but, after waiting a few moments, we uncovered her eyes; and I said, "Sadie, do you know me? Are you going to Jesus?" The dear child turned her eyes toward me, but was unable to utter a sound.

No sign could she then give to show whether or not she was happy; and soon her spirit took its flight, as we trust, to be with the Lord; for, although we could then have no word from her lips, we *mourn not* for her. We believe she had given herself to Jesus, and is now happy with him.

Shall I tell you something of this dear girl? She came to us last year from Cutturbul, near Diarbekir. She was about fourteen years of age, quite small and uncomely in form, but with a bright face, and lustrous black eyes. But we soon found that her bright face was *not always sunny;* for she had a very bad temper, and would often become angry at some word from her associates; and then her sunny face would be darkly clouded.

Kohar, our assistant teacher, often told us that Sadie was sometimes very troublesome, and even *hateful* to her associates. Much prayer was offered for this bright, wayward girl; and, after a time, she was awakened by the Holy Spirit, and led to see her sinfulness, and one sabbath day came to our room to talk about her soul. She felt that she was a great sinner, and earnestly inquired what she should do to be saved.

After we had explained to her the way of salvation, she felt that she could give herself to Christ, believing that he would forgive her sins, and give her a new heart. A few days after this, she told us, with a beaming face, that she had given herself to

Christ, that she gave her heart to him that sabbath day, and had since been *very* happy. Several times after this, she spoke of her joy and peace in Christ, and one day lingered at the close of a recitation, and requested me to give her some *spiritual advice*. I talked to her a few moments, when she looked up with a grateful smile, thanked me, and said, "I *wish* you would talk to me every day."

Miss Seymour spoke to her especially about looking to Jesus for strength to conquer her violent temper, and refrain from all angry words; and we believe she did indeed seek and find help from him; for, when she returned this year, she was much improved, and we feel that it was grace alone which had wrought such a change, that Kohar said of her, "She is *very sweet* this year."

Some weeks after her return, she came to

our room with a bright smile, to tell us of her love to Jesus, and ask us to pray that she might always live near to him, and be a blessing to others.

Soon after this, she was taken violently sick, and suffered much for nearly six weeks. We visited her several times, and always found her groaning with pain, but apparently trusting in Jesus. She requested us to pray for her, and wished to be remembered in the prayers of her schoolmates also.

Once I found her suffering greatly, and saying, "He will take me, he will take me." And when I said, "Sadie, do you *wish* to go?" her face instantly brightened, and she said, "Oh, yes!"—"But," said I, "you are a sinner. How can you go to heaven?"

She replied, "Yes: I am a *great* sinner, but *Jesus will save* me. It is only by Jesus, *only by Jesus.*"

At times she talked much of the preciousness of Christ, the joy of heaven, and her confidence in her Saviour; and I have never heard of any doubts of her acceptance, or fears of death, during the whole of her long sickness. At one time she said, "Since Christ has died for me, why should I not trust him? why should I fear death?"

One night she called her parents, and begged their forgiveness for all her unkindness and disobedience; and at another time, when asked if she was not sad in view of death, she said, "I am not sad when thinking of *myself;* but I grieve for my *parents.* I *know* it will be hard for them to bury me here, and go home alone."

Once she exclaimed, "I see the angels! they are coming for me." The day of her death, she was too weak to talk much; but, when asked if she would like to have prayers, she immediately said, "Yes."

Again, while suffering from intense pain, one asked, "Are you glad that the Lord has sent this upon you?" She said, "Oh, yes! glory, glory to thee, O Lord!"

These were her last words.

The next day we attended her funeral, and sang the sweet hymns, which Sadie had selected some days before,—"I want to be an angel," "Forever with the Lord," "I'm a pilgrim," "Come sing to me of heaven," and "Joyfully, joyfully." I doubt not you are all familiar with these same hymns, and perhaps often sing them, but not as we do here. Here they are sung in the Armenian language, and we have learned to enjoy them in this foreign tongue.

We felt that it was truly appropriate to sing, "Joyfully, joyfully," and that we ought not to *weep* for her, but should rather *rejoice* that Jesus had taken her from all the trials of earth, and especially that he had permitted her to give such good evidence of a change of heart, and fitness for the bright mansions.

And now, my dear young friends, may you all, like our dear Sadie, give your hearts to Jesus, ask him to make you his dear children, and give you strength to overcome all your faults, and grace to live for his glory. Give yourselves to Christ, *ask* him to guide you, and *believe* that he will do it. Do not be discouraged if you do not become like Jesus *at once*. Sadie did not immediately conquer, but was obliged to watch and pray as long as she lived, in order to keep down angry words and thoughts; but Jesus helped her, and has now taken her to himself, and given her the *crown promised* to those who *overcome*.

And so, dear young friends, he will *surely* help you, if you daily *ask* him to; and, if you cheerfully bear the *cross here*, he will give you the *crown* of life in *heaven*.

XXIV.

MISS M. E. WARFIELD.

ON the 16th of February, 1870, but a few weeks after penning the preceding letter, Miss Warfield followed her dear pupil, going up to wear "the crown of life in heaven."

Hers was a brief, earnest, effective missionary life of a little less than three years, spent in the Harpoot Female Seminary.

When the call came to engage in this work, though shrinking from its responsibilities, yet thinking the Master called, she cheerfully responded, "Here am I," and leaving the school which she was teaching in Arlington, Mass., prepared to bid farewell to her widowed mother and only sister, and go so soon as an associate should be secured. The proper person not being found so speedily as she had hoped, she fixed a time, delay beyond which in finding an associate should be to her evidence that she was mistaken in supposing her own call to be from the Master.

Telling her purpose to Him whom she loved to call the *dear* Saviour, she calmly waited that final *tenth* day, the evening of which providentially ratified her call by the news that Miss Hattie Seymour of Rochester, N.Y., would soon be ready to join her in her chosen work. Henceforth, whatever the thorns which beset her path, or the darkness which enshrouded it, in a work the peculiar difficulties and trials of which none in the home land, and few, if any, in the foreign field, besides the young ladies themselves, can fully appreciate, she never again gave place to a doubt that she had been divinely

MISS WARFIELD.

called, nor lost, for a moment, her cheerful zeal in doing her Master's bidding. She felt sure that he was with her, and would be to the end, though little suspecting how soon that end of earthly service was to come.

Her quick mind and enthusiastic earnestness secured for her a speedy and ready command of the language; and almost from the first day in the field she was a practical, efficient missionary. Her labor for her pupils was a cheerful service of love to them and her Saviour, — one in which no yielding to weariness or discouragement was allowed. The result was the condensation of an unusual amount of effective work into those brief months. Not content with their summer labors in the seminary, she and her associate devoted most of the winters to visiting their pupils in their places of labor, going for this purpose on horseback, through rain and snow, from outstation to outstation, some of them several days' journey distant. The return from these missionary tours usually brought a generous supply of cheer for the home-circle; for hers was a hopeful, buoyant spirit, not prone to look on the cheerless side of missionary life, but eagerly gathering up all which could energize herself or others for the work in hand. In these journeys, for the sake of economy in using sacred funds, she cheerfully bore some privations, which some of us older — shall I say wiser? — tourists have felt constrained to remand to the experiences of more youthful days. Returning from the last of these tours, made to several villages on Harpoot plain, she was taken with measles, which was prevailing in some of the places visited. Having a skillful physician at hand, we had no fear for the result, especially as the disease was in a mild form; but when, on the sixth day, typhoid-fever set in in a violent form, we felt that there was little hope.

Happily she herself had felt, days before, that her end was near, and, while yet in full possession of her reason, had left her dying-messages to her mother and other home-friends.

During the delirium of typhoid, she imagined herself called upon to suffer the martyr's death at the stake. Yet not even then did faith or courage fail; and it was touching to hear her exclaim, "Dear Saviour, thou knowest that I am weak, but do give me strength. I am willing to bear even this for thee." Recognizing her associate standing by her bedside, she exclaimed with all the earnestness of reality, "Go back, Hattie, go back! It is enough for one of us to die. You must stay, and bear witness for Christ."

The ruling thought was strong in death; and her whole anxiety was for the work and the people whom she came to bless, to imaginary companies of whom she was, from time to time, making earnest appeals on the one great subject.

And thus she went home to hear, no doubt, the welcome plaudit, "Well done!" and receive from her dear Saviour's hand the crown of that martyrdom she had consciously endured for him.

Her grave made the sixteenth in our little hillside cemetery; the first adult to lie there having been Mrs. Williams (Miss Barbour), who, though nine years before too modestly declining the post of first teacher in the seminary, had been providentially led hither to find a resting-place. And that burial-ground is not a sad place, — is really a "God's acre." Of all who lie there, we have the joyous assurance that they have entered into the rest which remains for the people of God.

What if their dust must, for a brief time, sleep far from that of their kindred and friends, among a people of a strange speech! This seeming isolation and loneliness will but make the angels watch all the more tenderly over it, till that day when *He* shall come to re-animate, and gather home, his chosen ones.

> " Asleep in Jesus, blessed sleep!
>   From which none ever wake to weep, —
> A calm and undisturbed repose,
>   Unbroken by the last of foes.
>
> Asleep in Jesus — oh, for me
>   May such a blissful refuge be!
> Securely shall my ashes lie,
>   And wait the summons from on high."

XXV.

THE MAN WHO MUST PREACH.

SOME time in the early days of our missionary life, a guest brought with him to our home, a young man, some twenty years of age, a native of the city of Égin, in the north-west part of our field. His large head, and somewhat larger self-assurance, with a good measure of aggressive force, and earnestly-avowed Protestantism, attracted our attention.

It was quite evident that he aspired to be a servant in the ministerial sense; for, complacently requesting the use of a small prophet's chamber, he, after a few days of seclusion, issued from it, manuscript in hand, with an invitation for himself to preach it from our pulpit on the following sabbath. This was our first acquaintance with Simon Deradoorian.

Soon after, he presented himself as a candidate for the theological seminary, to which he was received, and graduated with honor four years later, being remarkable chiefly for an excessive scrupulousness, and a strong tendency to asceticism; this last manifesting itself in the eating of some kinds of food which, though fitted, perhaps, to "bring under the body," are not fitted to develop a refined taste.

His earnestness and self-assurance did not fail; but the latter was somewhat discouraged by occasional exposure to ridicule, in his attempts to indulge it at the expense of those about him; as when a letter of private rebuke and exhortation to one of his teachers for a supposed fault was quietly passed along to be read and laughed at by the assembled students.

Alas that in the forceful application of the truthless as trite maxim, "Great men are always modest," the great, arrogant world so often blasts the blossoms of growing greatness! But the blossoming genius of our theologue was proof against even the withering influence of the "dread laugh" of the little world in which he moved, and upon which he looked down with the calm serenity of conscious superiority.

And the little world meanwhile repaid him with a certain sincere respect for his talents, and the ascetic rigor of his adherence to what he supposed to be right.

Gifted with a somewhat commanding presence, a good voice, and ready command of language, and giving due attention to the cultivation of the two latter, he was able, in his senior year, to take pre-eminence among his classmates as a preacher.

On graduating, he went to Temran, a

town among the mountains, to the north-east of Harpoot, in the then newly occupied district of Geghi. Though he there had no regular audience or place of worship, and so no opportunity to cultivate his preaching-talent, except occasionally in efforts to control crowds of excited hostile men, yet, in this primary evangelistic work, his natural earnestness, and his warm-hearted piety, found new nourishment, and opportunity to grow, and he profited by them. Those were the days of mobs in that wild district, in the midst of which he developed a, to us, new trait of character, — that of Christian mildness and forbearance, such as to win some of his bitterest enemies, and among them poor old Sarah, a sketch of whom is next given. She was one of a mob that threw his books and other possessions into the street, and beat him; but, seeing how patiently he bore it all, she exclaimed, " Poor young man, he don't deserve such treatment," and from that hour began to seek and love the truth for which he suffered. His brief stay there laid the foundation of a prosperous work, which is on the point of resulting in the formation of the second church in the district.

But here, as elsewhere, qualities and talents such as his are sure to win reputation in more important centers; and he soon received and accepted a call to Harpoot.

His course here was very brief; for he came only to die, being seized with typhus-fever ere he had preached a single sermon. But this new summons was received with the quiet confidence of one who knew in whom he had trusted. When told what would be the issue of his disease, and asked whether he felt afraid of death, his quiet reply was, "Why should the Christian fear to die?" And thus, in the vigor of his early manhood, and the beginning of his usefulness here, he passed away, to respond, we doubt not, to a call to enter upon a higher, wider sphere of usefulness in some other world.

> "Lift not thou the wailing voice,
> Weep not, 'tis a Christian dieth :
> Up where blessed saints rejoice,
> Ransomed now, the spirit flieth.
> High in heaven's own light he dwelleth;
> Full the song of triumph swelleth,
> Freed from earth and earthly failing :
> Lift for him no voice of wailing."

XXVI.

OLD SARAH.

SHE lived for seventy years in spiritual darkness in Temran, the town in which labored Simon Deradoorian, and then received her first ray of light from seeing the patience with which he endured the abuse of a mob, whom he blessed while they were beating him, and destroying his property.

She had gone with the crowd to see the "infidel preacher" beaten, — the man who did not worship the saints and the Holy Virgin, and who, of course, must be bad and behave very badly. But when she saw a meek, gentle Christian, who joyfully suffered for the Master's sake, her natural sense of justice was outraged by the violence of her companions; and she began to love the "good young man."

When Simon came to Harpoot, and died here, old Sarah attached herself to his successor, who, fortunately, was a man of kindred spirit.

A hard task had she before her in the effort to be a Christian; for, during all her adult years, she had been known, even in that wild, rough region, as a virago, — the terror of all who came in contact with her, men as well as women; for, in her terrible outbursts of passion, she hesitated not to enforce hard words with harder blows, when necessary for her purpose.

But, having made up her mind to serve Christ, she went to work with characteristic earnestness. Her little grand-daughter was at once put into the Protestant school; and when the new preacher and his wife came, taking the little girl upon her shoulders, she waded with them through the deep snows of that mountain-region to introduce them to the people at their homes. Happily, they were both earnest, spiritually minded people; and it was old Sarah's delight thus to go with them from house to house, and hear the "old, old story" told over and over again. The Bible was to her like a gushing fountain of pure cold water to one perishing with thirst. She never wearied of drinking in its sweet words.

Once, hearing the preacher read Christ's discourse with Nicodemus, she exclaimed, "Saviour, I am unclean! wash me with thy blood. There is no other way to be saved."

She seemed literally to hunger and thirst for the bread and the water of life; and, when the preacher went to visit another town, she was impatient for his return, saying, "Why does he not come?" and requesting those about her to talk to her of spiritual things. "Ah!" she exclaimed, "would that I had heard these things sooner!"

To the amazement of all about her, who wondered at the change, and admired the power of that gospel which was able to produce it, she became as remarkable for sweetness as she had before been for violence of temper.

Once only did the old nature get the better of the new, and then in a prayer-meeting, to hold which, some members of the Palu church had come three days' journey. A nephew of hers rising to leave in prayer-time, with the exclamation, "I don't accept your *groank*" (religion), she gave him a vigorous box on the ear, exclaiming, "You call prayer a *groank*, do you?"

But not long had she to fight the good fight of faith, only one winter's snows through which to wade to guide the preacher in his household visits. With the opening spring she sickened; and it was soon apparent that she was near her end. To the last, she clung to the place of prayer, saying, go she must. To some who once tried to dissuade her from going, she replied, "I must and will go to hear God's voice once more."

But three days before her death, she induced two men to take each an arm, and lead her to the loved place once more, for the last time.

The story of her death tells nothing of rapturous exultation, nothing of transporting visions of heavenly glory; but we doubt not she found an angel convoy in waiting to convey her thither. When wearied, and at times almost disheartened, by the worldliness and ingratitude of many for whom we labor, the memory of poor old Sarah wading through those winter snows, and trying to breathe her last breath in the atmosphere of prayer, cheers us with new confidence in the promise, "Lo, I am with you alway."

XXVII.

BÉGO, THE WIFE OF DONO.

BY REV. H. N. BARNUM, D.D.

IN the year 1868 twelve Protestant women in Palu, along with their family cares, secured each a few Armenian women and girls as pupils, hoping in this way to bring them into contact with the Bible. They rightly judged that this was one of the surest ways of doing good; for they themselves had recently learned to read, and, in learning, their minds had become awakened, and their hearts drawn to the truth.

Among these pupils was a bright married woman, less than thirty years of age, whose name was Bégo. She was much interested in reading, and made rapid progress. After a little, she removed, with her husband, to Temran, a village in the Geghi district, among the Anti-Taurus Mountains. This district is three days' journey from Palu, and surrounded on all sides by wild Koords. Soon after reaching Temran, following the example of the Palu sisters, Bégo opened her own house for the gratuitous instruction of such women and girls as were willing to come. There were very few such at that time, it is true; for this was a new thing in that region, and most persons regarded reading by females as very unwomanly. But it was the beginning of female education in a place which has already sent three girls to the female seminary in Harpoot. We heard of this school, and rejoiced in it as the shining of the light in a very dark place. None of us, however, saw the teacher; for she and her husband were faithful adherents of the old Armenian Church, and kept aloof from us.

Bégo's love of reading led her to study the Bible; and, as she studied it, the truth gradually dawned upon her mind, and she and her husband became convinced of the errors of the Armenian Church, and joined the feeble band of Protestants in Temran. I well remember the time when I first saw her. It was on a visit to Temran, in 1870. I was a guest of the preacher, when she timidly came in, and was introduced to me as the woman who was helping a few of her sex to read. She was not then openly committed to the truth; but, after a few months, she came out clearly and decidedly on the Lord's side.

Two years later (in 1872), in the midst of endeavors to do good, she was prostrated by a most painful attack of rheumatism, from which there is no hope of her recovery. On a recent visit to Temran, I called upon her. I was not surprised that she had rheumatism. The wonder is, considering the damp, cold houses the people live in, that so many of them escape this disease. The house which Bégo occupies is the ordinary one-story building, six or seven feet high, with mud walls, flat, earthen roof, and the bare ground for the floor. On one side, the whole length of the room, both the wall and the roof are so dilapidated, that they do not join each other, but leave an open space from three to eight inches wide. The room is bare of furniture, — a cheerless, comfortless place. Somebody has been sufficiently thoughtful, after she has lain for two years with her poor, hard mattress on the ground, to make a rude, wooden frame, and place her bed on that. At the foot of the bed, on the wall, hangs the recently issued roll of daily Scripture promises in Armenian, sent to her by one of the missionary ladies; and during the long, weary hours of the day, she comforts herself with these precious words. Her husband and little boy are kept at home from their shoemaking with sore eyes. As we enter, she appears a little embarrassed; for, with a woman's sensitiveness, she shrinks from the exhibition of poverty which her house too clearly manifests. We have seen many such dwellings before, and at once put her at her ease. A mattress is spread for us on the ground, with a soiled, tattered cover, — a very uninviting seat; but it is probably the best bed in the house. Before we left, we felt that we were sitting in heavenly places.

Here lies a woman in the prime of life. She is by nature unusually ambitious and enterprising. For two years, she has been the victim of a most distressing disease. At times her pain is so severe, that the approach of a person to her bedside brings from her an involuntary shriek, through the fear of being touched. Her muscles have become contracted and rigid. She can not move hand or foot. Her hands are so drawn in, and bent, that the fingers nearly touch the arm. She has not even the power to drive away the flies that swarm upon her face. She lies thus perfectly helpless, racked with pain, and able to sleep but little, even at night. Oh, how heavily the weary, weary hours and days and weeks and months must move along! Is patience possible in the midst of such suffering? How many could endure to lie helpless, and often for hours alone, like this poor woman, even if there were no suffering connected with it? Simply the flies and the fleas would make many people well-nigh frantic. But in the countenance before us is an expression which implies something more than mere patience. You do not need to ask whether she is happy. Joy beams through all her features,

— a heavenly peace, triumphant over suffering, such as is seldom seen in a human face. Yet happiness is so incompatible with such a wretched condition, without any alleviation, and with no hope of release, except by death, which may be many years in coming, that one can scarcely avoid asking the question which I did, "Can you be happy in this state?"

"Oh, yes!" she replied, "I am very happy. My soul is full of peace and joy. Jesus is present with me, and, although I suffer much pain, I want nothing more. Except for Christ's presence and blessing, I never could endure this. I am content to wait upon him, and let him do as he pleases. His will is the best."

This testimony was to me more assuring than all the philosophical demonstrations of the truth of Christianity. The Temran preacher says that he often goes to the bedside of this poor but blessed woman to have his own spiritual nature refreshed, and his faith strengthened. Bégo was to have been a Bible-reader in Temran; but I left her, feeling that she is doubtless doing vastly more for her Master by illustrating the power of the gospel to sustain one in trial, than she possibly could have done by the most active service, and possibly more than many a preacher or missionary. Seldom has a sermon impressed me so deeply, and I trust profitably, as the quiet, heavenly joy that beamed from the face of this humble disciple.

XXVIII.

THE AGED AUCTIONEER.

FAMILY BIBLES are of modern missionary introduction into Turkey homes, and so don't tell when the angels brought the ancestors of the rising generation.

On the plain, flat tombstone, then, of our patriarchal pilgrim is inscribed only, "*Died in* 1869;" for he himself used to say, as do most old people in this land, "God only knows when I was born." But, by the aid of certain historical landmarks located by him in his boyhood, we were able to infer, that some time during the reign of the famous but unfortunate sultan, Abdul Hamet, probably about the year 1780, the comely form of baby Garabed ("Forerunner") first gladdened the eyes of his father Harootune ("Resurrection") and his, to us, nameless mother, in their home in Gaban Maden, then the capital of the Harpoot pashalic.

His ancestral patronymic, Ockle Deryesian, which is not Armenian, but Turkish, and means "sea of wisdom," shows the estimation in which the family had been held by the Turks; but, as this reputation may have been the reward of paternal sharpness in auctioneering, we can not, unhesitatingly, adopt the old style, and assert that they were "poor, but honest." Honest, according to the Scripture, or even the Occidental standard, they surely were not; for no auctioneers are so in this land.

Young Garabed had fallen upon troublous times, even for troubled Turkey. His youth was terrified by the terrible janizaries, more pitiless in these then wild regions than in Constantinople, where the head of a "Christian dog" was cheaper than even that of the real animal.

His manhood saw the revolt against the attempt of Sultan Mahmoud to levy soldiers to supply the place of the exterminated janizaries, when the terrible Reshid Pasha made the streets of Maden run with the blood of hundreds, and, to increase the popular terror, impaled living revolters upon the different highways leading from the city, and pommeled the heads of others in huge stone mortars.

Older inhabitants still tell how they saw seventy heads cut off by a single yatagan, and the trunks thrown into the Euphrates; and that, on the third day after his impalement, one poor wretch transferred his girdle to his head to protect it from the rain.

It is an interesting fact, that from such scenes of horror, repeated in one form and another through his entire youth and early manhood, Garabed came out with his natural sensibilities unblunted, his heart still tender and sensitive as a little child's to sights or tales of suffering. It was this which made him eager to visit at once any sick person to whom he hoped to do any good, and which made him ever a welcome, because sympathizing visitor, to the sick and suffering Mohammedans, as well as to nominal Christians.

When the suppression of the revolt, and the transfer of the capital to Harpoot, began for Maden that work of decay which has reduced it from a flourishing city to a comparatively insignificant village, Garabed removed to this city, and continued the business which procured for him his surname, Talal ("Auctioneer").

When we read the inspired description of all our rising race, that "they go astray as soon as they be born, speaking lies," and remember that our Talal was not only brought up in the Orient, and with no Bible or religious teachings of any kind, and that auctioneers in this land go from house to house, and man to man, telling what preceding bids have been, and trying to get bigger ones, and that often the amount of their own commissions depends upon the amount of successful lying, we can easily imagine that our prospective saint had one very steep and long hill, " Difficulty," to ascend, before reaching the city whose gates exclude all liars.

Those who have not breathed from infancy an atmosphere of falsehood, whose very bones have not been pervaded and almost disintegrated by its poisonous effluvia, can never truly sympathize with the feebleness of those who, born, and having long dwelt, in this valley of the shadow of death, awake, at length, to an effort to escape from it, and rise to the pure air and crystal light of truth.

Then, too, the position of nominal Christians in this land, crushed for centuries beneath grinding Moslem oppression, is fitted to excite and strengthen a spirit of greed and parsimony, a "get-all-you-can, keep-all-you-get" disposition, which is second only to falsehood in its demoralizing influence on the soul. When it is remembered that our hero lived under the full power of these demoralizing influences, daily pursuing his business of auctioneering, for more than threescore years and ten, we may rely upon our readers to believe and bear in mind, without further repetition of the fact by us, that when, on the verge of his second childhood, poor old Talal first read the gospel terms, and learned, that, to be saved, he must first undo his life's work, he felt, and felt to the last day of his Christian pilgrimage, that his was a hard task,—one which only divine strength could enable him to complete. It will easily be believed that we, who thought we saw the strugglings of the new principle of Christian life within him, felt called upon to watch over and warm and nurse the poor old patient, much as a tender nurse would a cholera or typhoid patient just rising from the gates of death. We fed him carefully with the sincere milk of the Word, laid no very heavy burdens upon him, put his Christian integrity to no hard, rude tests, and hoped, to the last, that he was slowly fitting for those mansions which nothing unclean shall ever enter.

It was in 1855, on the arrival of Mr. Dunmore in Harpoot, that old Talal gained his first idea of simple, pure gospel truth, separated from its muddy admixture in the dead tongue and deader ritual of the Armenian Church.

He at once bought a primer, and learned to read, and, by his success, furnished a text for many a profitable sermon to the old, on their ability and duty to learn to read God's word; for the old man, who, for so many years had cried his wares through the streets of the capital, was known to almost everybody throughout the pashalic. And, having learned to read, he put his Testament and hymn-book, and, later still, a little book of prayers, into his bosom, from which he never removed them, except for sleep or reading, till his dying-day. And go past his little variety-shop when we might, — for, beginning the Christian life, he left off auctioneering as a business, — we saw him, if not serving a customer, serving himself from his bosom stores.

Unfortunately, his wife was too near a relative to her of poor old Job's or Socrates' home to encourage or help him at all in his

Christian pilgrimage: so he kept plodding on alone.

There was one employment for which, by his tall, erect, manly form, and his graceful bearing, as well as the respect felt for him by all, Armenians and Turks alike, he was peculiarly fitted, and in which he took both pride and delight,— that of being guide and body-guard to escort the missionary ladies going to hold female prayer-meetings in different and distant parts of the city. The delight came in, when, on arriving at the place of meeting, and carefully tying the donkey in a safe place, his age and known simplicity of character secured him admittance to the meetings themselves, no one objecting.

He apparently loved the place of prayer as well as did the good old deacon in Warren, Me., who, being asked how many were present at a certain meeting, replied, "Two,

Jesus and I; and we had a blessed time." He was seldom absent, never, except from illness; and when the feebleness of age bowed his tall form, and a local injury made it painful for him to sit, it was affecting to see him, in summer's heat and winter's cold, slowly and painfully, but with radiant face, making his way to the sanctuary, leaning upon his staff. We miss him sadly from his familiar place at the foot of the pulpit-stairs, so nearly beneath the sanctuary droppings, that no one else cares to fill the vacant place. When he could no longer walk as escort to the female prayer-meetings, we, at his request, provided him with a donkey to ride; and thus, up nearly to the time of his last brief illness, he enjoyed his coveted privilege. Never but once did any one venture, in his presence, to offer any disrespect to his *protégées;* and then he at once put himself in the path of the drunken Turkish soldier, and turned him aside.

In spirit and manner, he was a born and trained servant, such a one as our republican soil can not produce, nor our equality-loving citizens train, on any soil. The charge, that we missionaries spoil all our servants — or must I be more Occidental, and call them *help?* — by teaching them such republican notions that *we* serve rather than they, is, I fear, true in all cases except this one of Garabed, who came to our hands too old to be cured of any ways which were not anti-gospel. "On my head," was his uniform reply to every expressed wish, with a final "Any thing more?" at leaving, even when, as at times, he meant to have his own way, which was only in those very few cases in which he was sure he knew better than we how a thing ought to be done.

There are some vices — or must we call them virtues in such cases? — which even the gospel don't cure, but only renders them more inveterate. A conscientious, Christian bigot, one who means to compel all mankind to believe and do just right, and get to heaven in spite of themselves, is the most intolerable of all nuisances, one which can be expressed by but one word, — *pope*.

Now, happily, our Talal's bigotry, if such it can be called, didn't touch at all the domain of religion, and didn't reach the area of other people's activities. He only silently maintained sometimes his right to do his employers' work in his own way. He had, for instance, no respect for our fastidious prejudice against drinking from the same vessel with that "noblest of animals," the horse; and so, in spite of all our protestations, he continued to water horses, mules, and donkeys from our fountain bucket. This he continued to do till despair quickened our wits into curing one vice by another; and, appealing to his yet uncured love of money, we said, "Yes, it *is* easier to water the animals there: so we will forbid you no more. Go on, then, only letting us know how many bucketsfull they drink, and you shall have it for a piaster a bucket." The horses and we never again drank from the same vessel.

The old man was apparently inveterately addicted to the Oriental habit of smoking; and, while telling him it was harmful, we could not find it in our hearts to insist that he discard his pipe, except on our own premises, and particularly in the stable, which was then beneath our house.

But the good old man was sure he knew better than we that smoking was good for him, and, moreover, couldn't be harmful to our stable; and surely he who loved us so well could never do so naughty a thing as to set fire to our property. And so the dangerous habit was slyly indulged in the forbidden place, and no suspicious snuffings of ours, and declarations that there was the smell of tobacco-smoke, could convince *him* of the fact, till one day I scented out the yet burning pipe hid in a corner of the building. The offending thing was, of course, punished by being thrown into the street, and its master bidden to reflect on his part of the sin in thus *deceiving* us. This brief sermon on his besetting sin did its work; and he went home solemnly vowing to cut off the offending right hand. And he did it. Much to our surprise, he never smoked again, but became, from that day, an anti-tobacco apostle. Such was his zeal, that he composed a poem, copies of which he had written out, and put up in the two city churches, where others might read, and profit by his experience, when he should be gone. We give a nearly word-for-word translation of it, hoping that its wider publication may do good where the old man never expected it.

> "For many years tobacco's slave,
>   To it I've service done:
> Of money much I wasted have,
>   Advantage gaining none.
>
> E'en to old age, from boyhood's days,
>   I tribulation bore,
> Alas, for those my foolish ways!
>   But now my slavery's o'er.
>
> O boys! now fix your eyes on me,
>   And to my words give heed:
> You yet from it are wholly free:
>   Don't touch, don't smell, the weed.
>
> And brethren, you who love the stuff,
> And it habitually do puff,
> To your own selves you damage do;
> Try, gain the victory, I beg you.
>
> Why will you squander money so?
>   Break up all those chibouques!
> And cigarettes are worthless too:
>   Spend money for good works.

> This my brief life is nearly o'er,
> Soon shall I leave this earthy shore;
> Thus, as I to my fathers go,
> This my last counsel I leave you."

(Signed)   TALAL GARABED.

I have read somewhere a statement, that, in 1867, one religious denomination in the United States paid two million dollars for tobacco used by them, and left their missionary treasury seventy-six thousand dollars in debt.

Would that some one had given the statistics for other denominations! But one thing is sure. The Master keeps the account in his ledger; and if some Christians who spend more on tobacco in defiling God's air with its smoke, and — oh, tell it not in Gath; for not even infidel Turks do that — his earth with their nasty expectorations, than they pay for supporting the gospel at home and abroad, don't blush at meeting old Garabed in those pure mansions, it must be because divine compassion takes away there the power of shame for the follies and sins of earth.

The poor old man had one lifelong grief in the fact, that, in his home, he was alone in trying to live the Christian life. His wife, as before intimated, scolded him for his Protestant ways; his daughters were married to men (one of them a leading man in the city) who were far from the truth; and, of his two sons, the elder, in his tall manly figure the image of his father, had early gone to Constantinople as groom to the British ambassador, where he led any thing but a sober life; while the youngest, the Benjamin of the family, saddened his father's heart for a time by his vicious ways, and finally almost broke it by leaving him in his old age, and running away to the capital.

But these sorrows seemed only to make the poor old pilgrim cling the more closely to his hymn-book, his Testament, and his Saviour; developing more fully his child-like simplicity of Christian character. A sort of shrinking diffidence seemed to grow with his years and his Christian growth. Though possessing naturally quite a fine, sonorous voice, such was his apparent timidity in public prayer, that, when he "took part" in a meeting, the part became practically the whole to the rest of us, since, hearing not a word, we could only say amen in our hearts to the many good petitions he was supposed to offer. This was, in part, no doubt due to the sudden transition from the read, ritualistic church-service of threescore years and ten, in which he had been only a hearer and spectator, to the voluntary simple forms of Protestant worship.

As, however, he was elsewhere fearless and outspoken, we at one time hoped to make him useful as a traveling preacher, crying gospel-wares all abroad in his old auctioneer tones. But the attempt proved a complete failure. On his return from his first circuit, when asked what he had preached to the people, he replied, "Bak che gah, masoonk che gah, surpotes parehosootune che gah" ("There are no fasts, there are no relics, and no intercession of the saints"). And such had, in fact, been the substance of his crying aloud. Rescued in old age from the darkness of a system which made fastings, relic-worship, and calling on the saints the substance of Christian duty, and entering again among those still similarly benighted, his first impulse was to cry out against the clouds which were obscuring the Sun of righteousness. So we concluded that the good old man could preach Christ best by humbly living him at home. And this he continued to do, feebly and stammeringly at times, indeed, but still preaching him alike to all, both Mohammedans and nominal Christians, till at length, bowed by the weight of almost fourscore years and ten, he betook himself to his little upper room, and lay down upon his humble couch to witness for him once more by a peaceful Christian death. Yes, peaceful, *full of peace:* that's the word to tell all the story. As in life, so in death, there were no raptures, no exultings, but only a trustful, tranquil waiting for the Master's coming.

He loved to think and talk of the crystal walls, the pearly gates, and the golden streets; but he did it in much the same way as a sick child would talk of getting well, and going home once more.

He craved the privilege of burial, not in

Oriental style, but in a coffin, and begged us to sing at the grave, —

> "Joyfully, joyfully onward I move,
> Bound to the land of bright spirits above:
> Angelic choristers sing as I come,
> Joyfully, joyfully haste to thy home!
> Soon with my pilgrimage ended below,
> Home to the land of bright spirits I'll go:
> Pilgrim and stranger no more shall I roam,
> Joyfully, joyfully resting at home."

His wish was gratified, and, on the day of his burial, a larger crowd than at any funeral here before or since gathered at the Protestant church to do honor to the man whom all had known, and, in spite of his weaknesses, known only to respect and love. And, as we gazed upon his peaceful face, we thought of him as indeed joyfully resting at home.

At the head of the coffin sat his first-born, Jacob, who had returned from the capital in time to be welcomed by the old man's glad, warm embrace before he lay down to die. Since his father's death, he has begun to attend the Protestant service occasionally. Will not all who read this simple story offer at least one earnest petition, that both he and the yet absent Benjamin may return to their heavenly Father with the penitent prodigal's confession and prayer, and follow their father in the way to heaven?

XXIX.

PILGRIM ANNA.

ABOUT four years after the coming of Garabed, "the Aged Auctioneer," in Maden, to gladden the hearts of his parents, two other parental hearts, in a home some hundred miles north-east of the capital, were disappointed and saddened by the advent of "nothing but a girl," a portraiture of whom may make a good "companion picture" for that of old Talal, since, like him, she in mature life migrated to the new capital, where, in old age, she learned and received the simple gospel story, and, like him, went home, being about ninety years of age. During this time she had lived with a husband nearly half a century, and remained a widow thirty-three years. Her early life, like that of old Garabed, was passed amid scenes of oppression and violence, but among Koords rather than Turks. Like him, she was a person of tall, erect form, and graceful movements; but here the likeness ceases. While we could not surely certify to her uniformly conscientious truthfulness from the first, we can say, that if, during her later years, she ever told lies, it must have been some as the good old father of the faithful did,— when under very strong temptation. Nor was she apparently covetous.

The natural traits for which she was most noted were fearless energy, gratitude for favors received, and religiousness. The last made her devoted in performance of the rites and duties of the Armenian Church, and equally conscientious in acting up to her new found gospel light. Her fearlessness and energy are best illustrated by the fact, that when seventy years old, unattended by any one to care for her, simply hiring an animal in a caravan going thither, she set out upon a six-months' pilgrimage to the holy city, Jerusalem; which visit gave her the surname Haji ("Pilgrim"), the name which the Turks apply also to those of their faith who have paid their devotions at the sacred shrine in Mecca. We suggest, for the investigation of the curious, why it is that while Armenian males who have seen the holy sepulcher are called in their own tongue Mahdesee ("Seer of the death") as well as Haji, females receive only the Turkish appellation, one which is practically more honorable, as being in the ruling tongue.

We regret not having obtained the story of her journey from the mouth of the old pilgrim herself; but we can easily imagine most of the scenes in Jerusalem itself and the holy places about it, — the eager, ignorant, fanatical, frenzied devotion at the supposed sacred sites of the birth, the crucifixion, and the burial of our Lord, and the process of plundering in those dens of thieves hard by, the homes of the ecclesiastics. Her daughter, with an apparent unconsciousness of its wrongfulness, characteristic of those living under such a government, tells us of the tone of triumph with which the holy pilgrim, on her return, presenting her child with materials for a suit of clothes, exclaimed, "I bought these in the holy city, and hid them in my *shalvars* (Turkish trousers), and thus escaped paying duty at the gates, and have brought them so all the way." And on the way she alone of all the caravan escaped paying a tax in gross, levied near Damascus by the Arabs, who carried off horses and all, except the one on which she rode, which she put to his highest speed, and thus saved him to his owner, who, stripped of all his other possessions, reached Harpoot some time after her arrival here.

At another time, hearing a cry from a neighbor's house, she rushed in to find the master crying out in helpless distress because four gypsy women were robbing his house. The courageous crusader gave them all a sound beating, and sent them on their way.

She seems to have been of that rare class whose physical force is increased by anger. And, while giving her characteristics, we may as well whisper a confession, that, like the rest of us mortals, the good lady, both before and after the beginning of her saintly experience, did at times get angry, only, perhaps, a little oftener than some of us, and a little more so.

A characteristic story by a person at our elbow, illustrating this impetuous weakness, we refrain from telling, lest, to accidental ears, it pass at a premium. Suffice it to say, that, even in her later and more saintly days, our Haji had occasion often to recall the divine declaration, "He that is slow to anger is better than the mighty, and he that ruleth his spirit than he that taketh a city."

Almost immediately on the coming of Mr. Dunmore to Harpoot, she, with her daughter (wife of "God's Bedros") and family, attached themselves to the gospel party. Unfortunately, her perhaps waning courage and spirit were not equal to the labor of learning to read; and thus the Bible was to her *eyes* a sealed book. But it could not be such to her ears; for she was always glad when she could go into the house of the Lord. Of this privilege she seldom or never allowed herself to be deprived. Only a week before her death, when on a communion sabbath, on account of her feebleness, she was urged to remain at home, with the promise that the elements should be brought to her there, she refused, saying, "No! I will go on my own feet."

She was constant and frequent in secret prayer, so much so, that her daughter, who has the reputation of being less heavenly-minded, once said to her, "You go so often to your little room, that you will bring Jesus down into it." To which she replied, "He is my all."

But, though she loved much, she knew very little, if one can be said to do so who has heart-knowledge of Christ crucified. So little head and tongue knowledge had she, that she made three attempts before getting into the church, and then only got in because we who knew her decided that come in she must. Any questions about Christian doctrine soon bewildered her poor old head; and she would exclaim, "I'm only a poor old woman. I don't know any thing;" adding, one day, putting her hand upon her heart, "But I know I love Jesus."

So all doctrinal questions were dropped next time; and all the examination condensed into this, "Haji Anna, what do you hate most?"—"Sin."—"And whom do you love most?"—"Jesus." So, on this testimony of her tongue and life, she was welcome to the Lord's table; and no one repented of the step.

In the kindness of her heart, she prayed that her death might not take place in the winter, because then the sexton would suffer so much from cold in digging her grave in the rocky soil of the Harpoot cemetery. She had her wish, dying on the 30th of July. One more petition she asked of the Lord. She very much dreaded the physical death-struggle, and often said, "Lord, it will be hard to die. Be thou with me then." The dreaded struggle came not; for she died unexpectedly, as quietly as a child drops to sleep. During the few days of her illness, she frequently uttered brief ejaculatory prayers, such as, "Jesus, I have trusted in thee. Be with me." The day before her death, she suddenly called her daughter, who finding her much excited, and looking upward, inquired, "Mother, what has happened?" — "My brother Bedros came," she replied, referring to a favorite brother, who died about forty years ago. Shall we call all such seeming appearances of the loved and departed to the dying mere fancies? or are they sometimes but foretastes to the departing soul of the blessed companionships of the spirit-world? Do others than those whom Jesus loves and calls see such messengers from the yet unseen world to which they are departing?

Her last words were in token of gratitude to a little grandson, who brought her some grapes. "God bless the boy!" said she; and, without any sign of the near approach of death, instantly passed away, and passed, as we can not doubt, into the presence of him in whom she had trusted.

www.ingramcontent.com/pod-product-compliance
Lightning Source LLC
Chambersburg PA
CBHW030746230426

43667CB00007B/857